QUILTING
ILLUSIONS

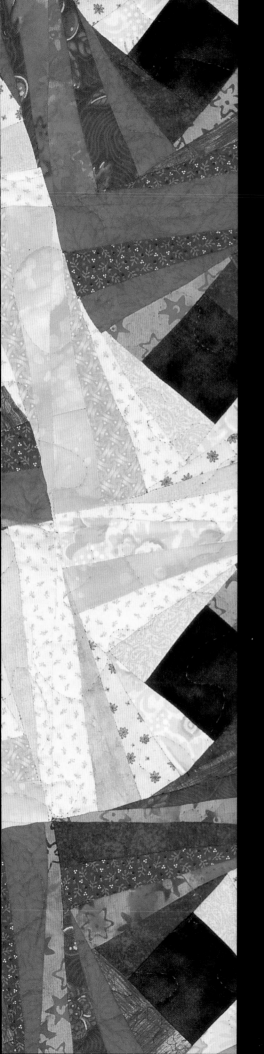

QUILTING
ILLUSIONS

CREATE OVER 40
EYE-FOOLER QUILTS

CELIA EDDY

BARRON'S

A QUARTO BOOK

First edition for North America published in 2004
by Barron's Educational Series, Inc.

Copyright © 2004 Quarto Inc.

All inquiries should be addressed to:
Barron's Educational Series, Inc.
250 Wireless Boulevard
Hauppauge, NY 11788
http://www.barronseduc.com

International Standard Book Number 0-7641-5677-2
Library of Congress Catalog Card Number 2003102239

QUAR.HEQ

Conceived, designed, and produced by
Quarto Publishing plc
The Old Brewery
6 Blundell Street
London N7 9BH

PROJECT EDITOR Paula McMahon
ART EDITOR Anna Knight
ASSISTANT ART DIRECTOR Penny Cobb
COPY EDITOR Sarah Hoggett
DESIGNER Tanya Devonshire-Jones
PHOTOGRAPHERS Ian Howes, Paul Forrester,
Martin Norris
ILLUSTRATOR Jennie Dooge
PROOF READER Sarah Hoggett
INDEXER Pamela Ellis

ART DIRECTOR Moira Clinch
PUBLISHER Piers Spence

Manufactured by Pica Digital Pte, Singapore
Printed by Star Standard Industries (Pte) Ltd, Singapore

9 8 7 6 5 4 3 2 1

CONTENTS

INTRODUCTION

There is a unique fascination in looking at two-dimensional images that deceive us into seeing something that isn't really there—a magical quality that at once teases and enchants the eye. Optical illusion has been a feature of visual art in all cultures and through all ages. Quilters have exploited ancient patterns and developed their own designs for as long as quilts have been made. They even have their own special name for them—"eye-fooler" quilts.

It was not until 1971 that the amazing graphic effects achieved by the American quilters of the nineteenth century began to gain the recognition they deserved. That year, the collectors Jonathan Holstein and Gail van der Hoof mounted the first ever display of quilts in an art gallery, at the Whitney Museum of American Art in New York City. The exhibition was called "The Pieced Quilt: An American Design Tradition." Here, for the first time, people were able to see and appreciate these magnificent works of folk art in the same setting and in the same way as paintings. When quilts came off beds and were put on walls, it became evident that many patterns appeared to mirror the effects seen in modern art, with one difference: Most of these quilts were made by women in domestic situations well before the development of any modern art movement. Most of the exhibited quilts' makers had no knowledge of or exposure to fine art of any sort, let alone the works of modernism. The optical illusions that emerge from so many of these quilts may have been unplanned, but they are nonetheless remarkable for that.

OPTICAL ILLUSIONS AND HOW THEY WORK

Although quilts made from patterns that deceive the eye have a special fascination, the patterns themselves are not necessarily complex or difficult to create. The effect of complexity stems purely from the way in which the pattern elements and colors work together in an overall design. Optical illusion can be created in several ways, and in this book we look at six of the most common: perspective and 3D, circles, grids, interlacing, counterchange, and transparency.

The illusion that a surface that we know to be two-dimensional *looks* three-dimensional, or that we seem to be looking at layers, produces some of the most intriguing and satisfying effects in quilt making. The eye is fooled into seeing depth, perspective, and shadows, producing exciting and complex effects that, quite literally, lift the quilt surface into another dimension. How does this happen?

Three-dimensional effects—Fans in Boxes and Scrap Boxes.

PERSPECTIVE AND 3D

In a three-dimensional design, objects seem to have solidity and sometimes even to float over a flat surface. Three-dimensional illusions are created in quilt making in exactly the same way as in painting—through the use of light and dark tones. Imagine the façade of a building lit by bright sunshine, while one side of it is in deep shadow. Both sides are made from the same material and are, therefore, the same color—but in a painting, the only way to make the illusion look convincing is to make the shadowed side much darker in tone. Exactly the same principle can be used in quilt making. A classic example of this is the Tumbling Blocks pattern, a popular pattern for traditional quilts, in which cubes appear to stand out from the surface; the contrast between light, medium, and dark fabrics produces the illusion. Another example is Right-Angle Patchwork, in which a series of boxes seems to be piled up one on the other. Again, the three-dimensional effect will appear every time, provided the colors are correctly shaded. Other patterns, such as stars, can produce a faceted effect, achieved by the simple juxtaposition of certain shapes and colors.

Perspective gives the impression that an object is viewed at a distance or has depth. There are several ways for quilters to achieve these effects, some of which are shown in the project quilts. In some, such as Scrap Boxes, the impression of depth comes from using mitered frames and black for the bottoms of the boxes. In other quilts, such as Attic Windows, the illusion of depth is created by juxtaposing two shapes in different tones and joining them by a diagonal line, to create a "frame."

CIRCLES AND CURVES

Many traditional American quilt blocks, when repeated, create the illusion of interlocking circles over the entire quilt surface. Others reveal a series of curves and arcs. This effect seems all the more mysterious when one realizes that the blocks are constructed without any curved seams. In fact, the secret lies in very simple geometry and results from the juxtaposition of certain angles. Because they are close to each other, the eye automatically sees them as being related and, as it were, "fills

Pieced triangles create the
Kaleidoscope illusion.

in" the missing sections of the circle so that we are deceived into seeing them as joined. These are some of the most satisfying patchwork patterns, as the piecing is often very simple but the effects can be stunningly complex. There are a number of patterns that play on this illusion: Kaleidoscope quilts are the outstanding example, but there are others, such as Storm at Sea and Road to Paradise. A slightly different technique, using only straight lines, also results in an impression of curves and swirls over the quilt surface in the pattern known as Twisted (or Revolving) Log Cabin.

GRIDS

Grids give the illusion that we are looking at layers. Many grid patterns are created by setting blocks with sashing strips; as with all eye-fooler quilts, the key is to make sure that the sashing strips contrast strongly enough with the blocks. Some blocks contain shapes within themselves that result in the appearance of a grid when they are repeated side by side; Railroad Crossing and Country Roads are examples.

of these patterns, the choice of color is vital to the success of the design, many of which would otherwise lack interest as the shapes would merge together. Take, for example, Kentucky Chain. With only two colors, a pattern still emerges, but there is no illusion of interlacing.

COUNTERCHANGE

The principle underlying counterchange is that positive and negative shapes and colors can be interchanged. Many of the designs of the artist M.C. Escher are based on this principle. At first one color or shape seems dominant, but the eye soon sees an alternative interpretation of the pattern. Indiana Puzzle is a perfect example of this. In some patterns, two completely different shapes may vie for attention, in which case the same pattern can produce two entirely different quilts when the respective light and dark values are exchanged. This is what happens with Star Cross, in which one is first convinced that there is only one shape; then the focus shifts and the other shape becomes dominant.

TRANSPARENCY

In transparency the illusion is created that one fabric is physically laid over another, with the underlying fabric showing through to the surface. There are three main ways of creating the effects of transparency: You can choose two colors plus a darker version of one of them (or black) for the area where they appear to overlap; you can use colors that are next to each other on the color wheel (analogous colors) in such a way as to suggest overlapping; or you can use as your "overlap" color the color that is created by physically mixing together the other two colors in your quilt (for instance, blue and yellow mixed together make green; therefore, using blue and yellow in your quilt, with green in the overlap patches, will suggest transparency).

Grids affect the pattern itself in sometimes surprising ways. A very simple block can look more complex and interesting when it is placed within a grid format, as the eye is fooled into seeing the underlying shapes as being related to each other. In Latticed Squares, for example, the grid gives the impression that a pattern has been squashed or flattened under it, as in Harvest Sun, where a simple fan block placed within a grid gives the impression of radiating sun rays. Other blocks, like All Kinds, achieve much greater interest and complexity when another block appears to be lying beneath the grid.

INTERLACING

Interlaced lines and shapes are decorative features in many cultures and traditions. From ancient Celtic knot patterns to the geometrically complex Moorish designs seen on tiles and screens, they tantalize the eye as they weave in and out, over and under. These illusions are seen to wonderful effect in several traditional patchwork patterns and blocks, and are a constant source of inspiration to contemporary quilters. Some of the simplest patterns can produce striking results. What could be easier than the well-known Rail Fence, which consists of nothing more than strip-pieced bands that are cut up and rearranged? Nine-Patch Weave, a very simple patchwork block, achieves greater interest and complexity purely by the placement of shapes and colors. Indeed, in most

HOW TO USE THIS BOOK

Each project in this book includes information on how to draft the pattern, suggestions for fabric colors, and step-by-step piecing instructions.

The necessary templates are shown in each project, and you can follow the detailed instructions for drafting blocks and patterns on pages 20–23. These instructions will enable you to draft blocks and patterns in whatever size you choose.

The colors used in each project are merely an example; the final decision is up to you. But if the shades or tones of colors are important to the illusionary effect, it is noted in the text, so that you can choose fabric colors within those ranges.

SEAM ALLOWANCE

Note that, unless otherwise stated, you need to add a ¼-inch (6-mm) seam allowance to all templates and other measurements and that all blocks and quilts are sewn with a ¼-inch (6-mm) seam. The exceptions to this are English patchwork and fusible webbing appliqué, where the templates are made to the finished size without adding a seam allowance.

MAKING THE QUILT

Once you have decided on a pattern that you want to make, draw the block full size and color it. Alternatively, make a scaled-down drawing of the block, and photocopy it several times so that you can try out different color groups until you're satisfied with your choices.

Make the templates, following the instructions on page 21.

Now choose your fabrics, following the guidelines for tones and shades if these are given for your chosen pattern. Cut out the patches, and follow the step-by-step instructions to construct the block. Some of the blocks are constructed as a series of units, which are then joined; speed up the sewing process by making up each set of identical units at the same time.

The Attic Windows pattern is a popular patchwork quilt.

Each quilt project is introduced with a photograph.

Detailed diagrams show the drafting method for the block used, from which you can identify the templates to make.

Follow the step-by-step instructions to piece the block in the units shown.

Follow the diagrams to complete the block as shown.

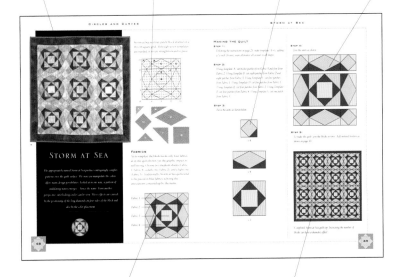

Suggestions are given for color choices when appropriate.

Each quilt and variation is colorfully illustrated.

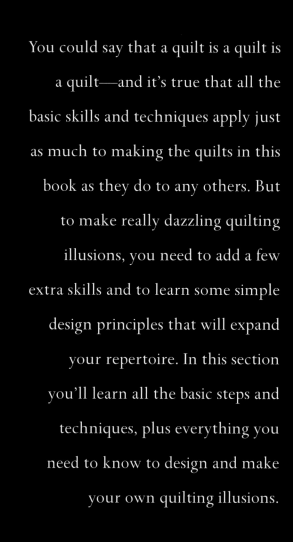

How to Make a Quilt

You could say that a quilt is a quilt is a quilt—and it's true that all the basic skills and techniques apply just as much to making the quilts in this book as they do to any others. But to make really dazzling quilting illusions, you need to add a few extra skills and to learn some simple design principles that will expand your repertoire. In this section you'll learn all the basic steps and techniques, plus everything you need to know to design and make your own quilting illusions.

TOOLS AND EQUIPMENT

Everything you need for quilt making, from drafting and designing to quilting and finishing, is listed here. There are many more aids and tools available from specialist suppliers, but these are the indispensable ones. Of course, one person's useful tool may be another person's useless gadget, so don't be afraid to try out other pieces of equipment just because they're not mentioned here. Aim to buy quality equipment, even if it's a little more expensive. In the long term, you'll find that it's money well spent and you will save a lot of time and frustration.

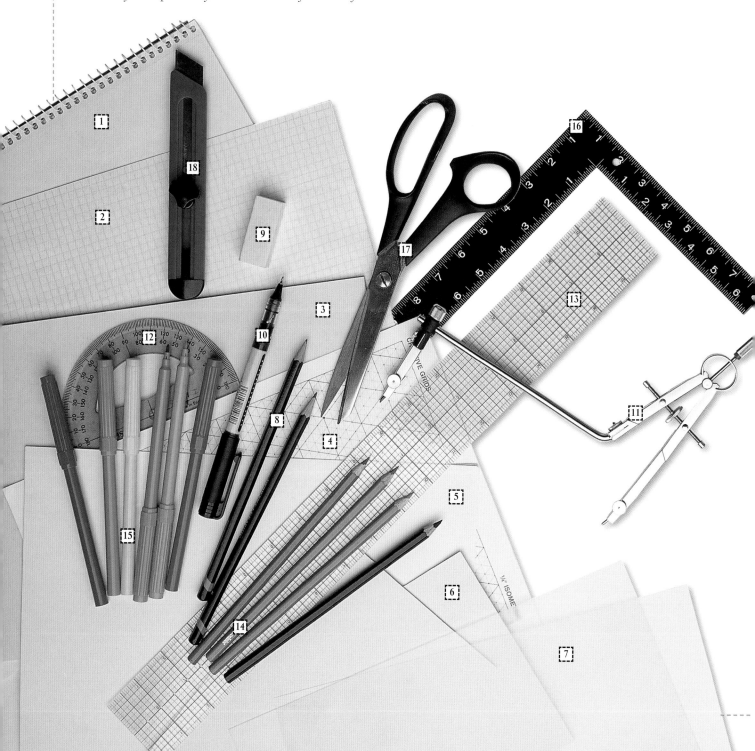

DRAFTING AND DESIGN

For drafting and design, you will need all the
following items, most of which can be obtained from
any good arts and crafts retailer. Again, invest in
quality and update your supply regularly.

1 *Drawing paper for drafting full-size*
   blocks
2 *Graph paper*
3 *Tracing paper*
4 *Isometric paper, which is marked in*
   triangles, for drawing hexagonal patterns
   such as Tumbling Blocks and other
   patterns, such as six-pointed stars, that
   are based on 60-degree triangles.
5 *Heavy quality paper for English*
   patchwork
6 *Cardboard or mounting board*
7 *Template plastic, including gridded, if*
   available.
8 *HB (semi-hard) and 2B (soft) graphite*
   pencils
9 *Eraser*
10 *Fine-point black ink drafting pen*
11 *Compass with extension bar, for drawing*
   extra-large circles and curves
12 *Protractor to measure angles and draft*
   triangles
13 *Acrylic ruler at least 15 inches*
   (22.5 cm) long x 2 inches (5 cm) wide
14 *Good-quality colored pencils*
15 *Fiber-tip pens*
16 *Metal ruler*
17 *Paper scissors*
18 *Craft knife*

COLOR VALUE FINDERS

Viewers are invaluable for evaluating color values during
the design process. Use all or any of the following:

19 *A reducing glass, which shows how your fabrics or quilt will look*
   from a distance and how well the color values will work. You can get
   the same effect by looking through the wrong end of binoculars.
20 *A multi-image lens—a Perspex (acrylic) sheet, through which you*
   can see how one block will look when multiplied, and also how the
   quilt will look from a distance.
21 *A Value Finder—a red lens that eliminates color but reveals value*
   (that is, the relative dark and light tones). Note: the Value Finder is
   not effective for use with red fabrics.

COMPUTER PROGRAMS

Computer users can use some of the many available
graphics programs to create original quilt designs. There are
also some dedicated quilt programs available now, which
make quilt design easy and fun. You can draft blocks
yourself or use the blocks in the libraries, which the
currently available quilting programs all contain. Blocks
can be changed, resized, and colored, and then set into
quilts. You can design quilts and arrange sizes and layouts.
Some programs calculate the quantities of fabric required
for any particular project and let you print templates of the
required size. These programs are an invaluable design
resource and save a great deal of time.

CUTTING FABRIC

Good, sharp cutting tools are essential. Get your scissors sharpened regularly and never use your fabric scissors for cutting paper or cardboard. Rotary cutter blades need to be replaced regularly, although some firms offer a sharpening service.

1 *Large fabric scissors. Look for a pair with spring-loaded handles, which are easier to use—especially if you have hand or wrist problems or want to avoid them.*

2 *Rotary cutter and mat—ideal for speedy cutting of patches and strips and trimming finished blocks. A useful average size of mat for general purposes is 17 x 23 inches (43 x 58 cm). Cutters come in various sizes, but the most commonly used has a 1¼-inch (3-cm) diameter blade.*

3 *Specialized acrylic ruler, 24 x 6 inches (60 x 15 cm), for use with rotary cutter and mat.*

4 *Acrylic square 12½ x 12½ inches (30 x 30 cm), for cutting squares of all sizes and squaring up blocks.*

SEWING

Having the right sewing equipment will enable you to achieve quick, accurate piecing and construction. If you use a sewing machine, carry out regular basic maintenance, removing lint from around the bobbin and following the manufacturer's instructions for cleaning and oiling.

1 *Small, sharp scissors for snipping threads and trimming corners. Use these, rather than your large fabric scissors, for small jobs to save the latter from becoming blunt.*

2 *Seam ripper for unpicking stitches and for any other job requiring a small, sharp point.*

3 *Metal tape measure for accurate measurement of large items, such as quilt tops.*

4 *Ordinary dressmaker's pins for small patches.*

5 *Long, glass-headed pins for larger patches.*

6 *Extra long, fine glass-headed pins for pinning quilts together.*

7 *Flat-headed (or flower-headed) pins for pinning patches that are to be machine sewn together. They can be left in as you sew because they are especially fine and the needle can run over them without damage.*

8 *All-purpose needles in a variety of sizes for basting and for hand-sewing patches.*

9 *Specialized needles for hand quilting, called "betweens." Betweens come in sizes from about 5 to 12, with 12 being the smallest and finest. For most purposes, size 9 or 10 will be suitable.*

10 *Good-quality machine thread. Cheap thread is a false economy, as it may disintegrate in the seams and cause your patchwork to come apart or it may break or snag in the machine.*

11 *Quilting thread for hand quilting.*

12 *Embroidery thread and metallic thread for embellishment.*

13 *Ordinary metal thimbles for basic sewing.*

14 *Metal thimble with ridge around the crown for hand quilting.*

15 *Finger guard (usually made of leather) for protecting the finger that is held underneath the quilt during quilting.*

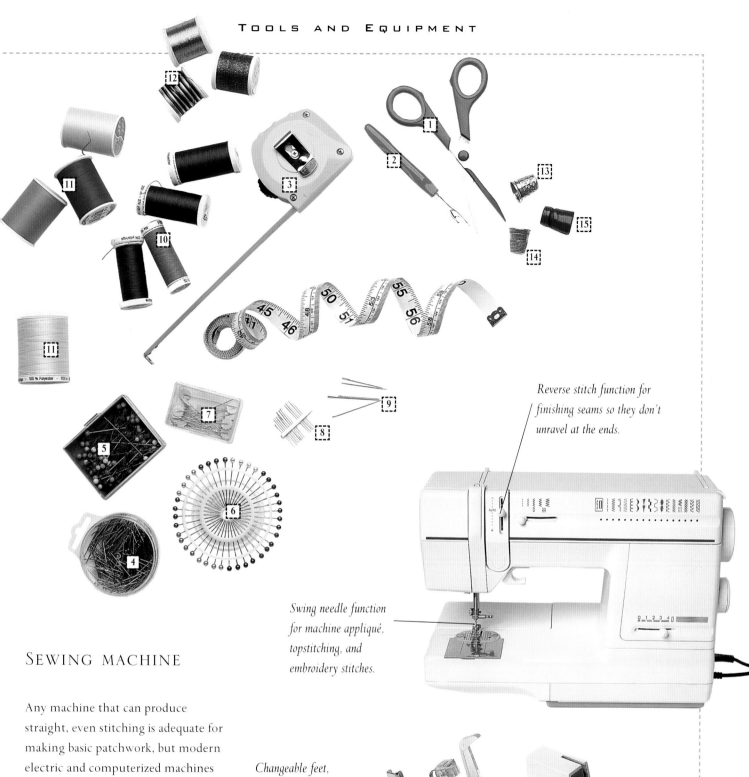

Reverse stitch function for finishing seams so they don't unravel at the ends.

Swing needle function for machine appliqué, topstitching, and embroidery stitches.

SEWING MACHINE

Any machine that can produce straight, even stitching is adequate for making basic patchwork, but modern electric and computerized machines provide many other useful features. If you're thinking of investing in a new machine, it's useful to know about these. The features that I find the most useful are as follows:

Changeable feet, including a darning foot and an embroidery foot. A foot with an automatic ¼-inch (6-mm) measurement is ideal for sewing accurate seams.

Feed dog cover plate, or device for dropping the feed dog, used for free machine quilting.

Walking foot, also known as an even-feed foot—a special attachment for machine quilting.

ASSEMBLING AND FINISHING QUILTS

At the final stages of the quilt-making process, you will need to make many choices about layout, quilting, and how to finish the edges. For quilting, you may need to try out several possibilities before deciding which equipment suits your purposes best. Don't buy a large frame, for example, until you've had a chance to try working on one, either in a shop or by borrowing one from a friend.

1 *Floor frame, if you have the space.*
2 *Large quilt hoop for bed quilts and large items.*
3 *Smaller quilt hoop for smaller items.*
4 *Stencils and templates for marking quilt designs.*
5 *Light box (optional)*
6 *Masking tape*

MARKING QUILTING PATTERNS ON FABRIC

Mark light fabrics with dark pencils or special quilt-marking pencils—a 2B (#2) pencil can be rubbed off easily when quilting is finished. For darker fabrics, try light fabric markers, such as white quilt-marking pencils, which can also be easily removed. A permanent ink pen, such as a Pigma pen, can be used for making permanent labels for the backs of quilts.

7 *Quilter's silver pencil, fine-point permanent ink pen, 2B (#2) lead pencil, and a white quilt-marking pencil.*
8 *Fabric eraser*

Batting to place between quilt top and backing

There are several types to choose from:

9 *Polyester. Polyester batting is available in several weights: 2 or 4 ounce (50 or 100 g) will work provided it is of good quality. Some cheaper versions "beard"; that is, the fibers migrate through the quilt top, creating a fuzzy effect. Always ask the retailer about this before purchasing.*

10 *Needle-punched polyester. This is thin and dense and does not usually beard.*

11 *Wool. Wool is expensive, but it gives unrivaled warmth and is very easy to quilt.*

12 *Cotton. Cotton batting comes in various weights and qualities and is particularly effective in producing the look and feel of a traditional quilt. Mixed cotton and polyester battings are good value.*

Fabrics

13 *Cotton patchwork fabrics.*

14 *Backing or lining: muslin or other pure cotton fabrics.*

15 *You can use more exotic fabrics, such as satin and silk, but you may need to stabilize them with lightweight interfacing or fusible webbing.*

Other useful equipment

Contemporary quilters are fortunate in having many tools to make life easy. Here are some examples.

16 *Fusible webbing is useful for appliqué. It comes on sheets of paper on which shapes can be drawn and then cut out.*

17 *Freezer paper, also used for appliqué, is thick, white paper that is slightly sticky on one side. It can be ironed onto fabric with a hot iron and will adhere. It can be peeled off easily after the sewing is complete.*

USING COLOR IN QUILTING ILLUSIONS

Color is an important element in many quilting illusions. Some illusions, such as grids and layers, achieve their effect through well-contrasted colors, while others, such as Tumbling Blocks, achieve their effects through different tones of the same color. For this reason it's useful to have some idea about how colors work together. Although color theory can get very technical, a few basic principles will help you choose colors to enhance illusionary effects without getting too bogged down in the detail. If you want to know more about this fascinating subject, there are several excellent books, some of which you'll find in the Bibliography on page 128. You'll find suggestions for use of color values in the projects.

The first step is to familiarize yourself with the color wheel, which demonstrates the relationships between colors. There are three primary colors—red, blue, and yellow. Secondary colors—green, orange, and violet—are made by mixing together any two primaries. Between these colors, as you'll see, there is an infinite gradation of colors.

Colors that are opposite each other on the color wheel are said to be "complementary" to each other—for example, red and green, or orange and blue. Using those colors together usually results in clear contrasts. Colors that are near each other on the color wheel are described as "analogous." An example is red-orange, orange, and yellow-orange. Analogous colors are used to create harmony and the impression of unity.

It's helpful to know some basic color terminology, as you will probably come across these terms in books and projects.

HUE *simply describes and names the color as it appears on the classic color wheel: red, violet, or green, for example.*

INTENSITY *describes the brightness, depth, and impact of the color.*

SHADES *are dark values of a pure color, resulting from the addition of black.*

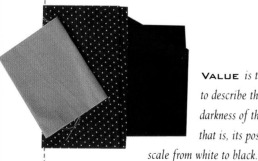

VALUE *is the term used to describe the lightness or darkness of the color— that is, its position on a scale from white to black.*

TINTS *are light values of a color, achieved by the addition of white.*

TONES *are color values achieved by adding values of gray (produced by mixing black and white with the pure color).*

Colors are often described by temperature. Some (reds, browns, purples) are said to be in the "warm" range, while others (blues, greens, violets) are said to be in the "cool" range. The color wheel shows which colors are grouped together and where the different ranges merge into each other. Understanding this can help you set a mood or style for a quilt. A quilt with a winter theme might use cool blue and white colors, for example, whereas a quilt celebrating summer might contain a range of reds, yellows, and oranges.

Contrast—the relative darkness and lightness of colors—is also important. The most dramatic example is black contrasted with white. Note that dark colors tend to advance toward the eye, and light ones tend to recede. This effect may influence the balance of the pattern.

Yellows

Greens

Oranges

Blues

Reds

Purples

The color wheel

HOW TO SELECT COLORS FOR A QUILT

Once you've decided on the general effect you want to create, you need to choose fabrics and colors to enable you to realize your idea. The most important first step is to arrange a space where you can pin up work in progress and view it from a distance. If you have the space, fix a large piece of foam core or corkboard to the wall and cover it with white felt. Otherwise, improvise by affixing a white sheet to a door or other surface. You will also need one of the viewing tools described on page 13, which will let you see how the fabrics will look from a distance.

There are several methods of choosing fabrics and colors. One way is to decide on your colors first and then find the fabrics to match them. For this, a set of paint chips (the sort you get at home improvement stores) is invaluable. You can use them to mix and match colors until you arrive at a combination you think will work, and then choose fabrics to

match those colors as closely as possible. The *Designer's Guide to Color* books are a good resource. They offer guidance on which colors go together and how they relate to each other.

Another method is to pull colors from a fabric that you've already selected. This method was used for Attic Windows on page 50, which starts with the busy pansy print. Fabrics that echoed the colors in the print were then used. This method ensures that the colors won't clash with one another and will unify the color scheme.

The way we perceive colors is affected by their context. You can use this knowledge to affect the overall look of a quilt. For example, if you put a red border around a scrap quilt comprising many colors, the reds in the quilt will stand out more. Add a blue border and the blues will appear dominant.

Another way to give your quilt a coherent look is to choose one of the prepackaged sets of coordinated fabrics now available. They usually include solid-colored fabrics, and large and small prints, checks, and stripes, and you can supplement the set by adding your own fabric choices.

As a last step, draw an outline of the pattern on cardboard, snip small pieces of the selected fabrics, and pin them to the positions in which they will be used. Fix the cardboard to your viewing space and see how the colors look. When you're happy with the way the colors work together, lightly glue them to the cardboard and keep it for reference as you work.

A LAST WORD ABOUT COLOR

In the end, what works is what *you* like. Sometimes departing from the accepted ideas of what you should and shouldn't do can result in the most striking and successful quilt. Go to any quilt show and you will soon see how often this is true!

DRAFTING PATTERNS AND MAKING TEMPLATES

Many ready-made templates for particular patchwork patterns can be purchased, and you can also buy sets of templates in different shapes and sizes. These are very convenient and timesaving, and have the added advantage of being 100 percent accurate in their measurements. However, there are times when you want to make patterns for which ready-made versions are not obtainable. This is usually the case when you're designing your own patterns and quilts. So, you'll need to be able to draft patterns yourself and make your own templates. Spend a little time learning the basic techniques and you will be able to apply the same principles to any pattern or design. Soon you will be able to express your own ideas and realize in fabric any design that your imagination can devise.

DRAFTING WITH GRIDS

Most patchwork blocks can be drafted on square grids. The conventional way of categorizing blocks is according to the type of grid used; for example, four-patch blocks are drafted on grids that are either 4 x 4 or multiples of four. This system makes drawing patterns easy once you've identified the category of the block. You can scale up or down to any size you want. However, not all blocks are drafted on square grids; so other types of grids for drafting will be dealt with in this section. How to tackle patterns needing special treatment, such as curves and circles, will also be explained.

Equipment for drafting and designing templates.

SQUARE GRIDS

Follow this sequence when drafting on square grids:

STEP 1

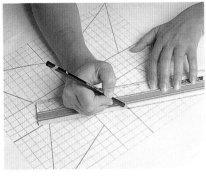

On drawing paper, draw a square (or other shape) of the size you want your block to be and draw a grid. You'll see that for each project that can be drafted on a grid of squares, the number of lines for the grid is given. For example, King David's Crown is a simple four-patch block needing a grid 24 x 24. Draw in the lines of the pattern.

STEP 2

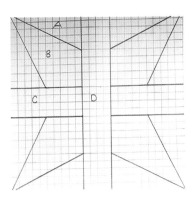

Use a black marking pen to go over the grid lines. Identify the different shapes in the block and mark them A, B, C, and so on. The diagram shows a simple four-patch block, but the method can be applied to any block.

TEMPLATES

This method can be used for all templates:

STEP 1

Cut out each shape using paper scissors and glue it onto cardboard or template plastic. Using a ruler and a sharp pencil or marking pen, draw a line around the whole shape exactly ¼ inch (6 mm) beyond the edge of the shape. This line marks the seam allowance.

STEP 2

Cut out the shape on the line, using sharp scissors or a craft knife. If you're working on heavyweight cardboard, use a metal ruler and hold the knife straight up from the side of the ruler. Use labels to identify the shapes on template plastic. Pen and pencil marks don't show up well on plastic and can be rubbed off.

• **TIP** Labels also keep the templates from becoming invisible when you misplace them on your work table or when they fall on the floor!

ISOMETRIC GRIDS

The most common alternative to the square grid is based on 60-degree diamonds. It is usually referred to as an isometric grid, and it is useful for drafting any pattern that involves 60-degree angles or multiples thereof. All hexagon patterns are based on this grid, as well as several others that you'll find in the projects in this book. The following are some examples of patterns drafted on an isometric grid: Oriental Star, Right-Angle Patchwork, Tumbling Blocks, and Six-Pointed Star. Follow the lines on the grid to draw in the pattern. Use the method described above for making the templates.

Oriental Star

Right-Angle Patchwork

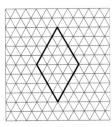

Tumbling Blocks

Six-Pointed Star

DRAFTING CIRCLES AND CURVES

Lots of interesting curved-patch blocks and patterns can be drafted using a compass. Traditionally, circles and curves were drawn around whatever domestic items came easily to hand, such as plates, saucers, and cups of the appropriate sizes. You can still follow this method if you like, but there are some simple mathematical ways of drafting, which can be applied to several blocks.

The following instructions are for some of the basic designs used in the projects in this book. To make the instructions clear, measurements are given for drafting to a specific size, but you can increase or decrease this size by adjusting the measurements proportionately. For this sort of design, you need good-quality drawing paper, pencils, a compass, a protractor, and a ruler. For curved seams that are to be pieced, you need to draw in a series of marks at regular intervals on the curve and transfer these marks to the templates. The marks are also marked on the patches to act as guides when you join the curves.

The tools below are used when making a block with curved seams.

TO DRAFT ROBBING PETER TO PAY PAUL

The measurements given here are for a 6 x 6-inch (15 x 15-cm) block.

STEP 1

Draw an accurate 6-inch (15-cm) square.

STEP 2

Find the center by drawing diagonal lines from corner to corner.

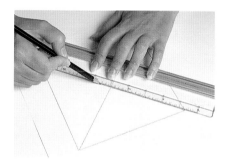

STEP 3

Draw lines through the center of the square from side to side. (You will need either a protractor or a ruler with clearly marked right-angle lines on it to do this.) Extend one of the lines exactly 3 inches (7.5 cm) beyond the edge of the square.

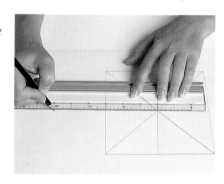

STEP 4

Place the point of your compass on the end of the extended line. Open it to 4 inches (10.5 cm) and draw an arc from corner to corner of the square. This arc is the template for the block. Trace it and transfer it to cardboard or template plastic. Remember, if you're using the template for the fusible webbing appliqué method, you do not need to add a seam allowance around the template.

TO DRAFT A MELON PATCH PETAL

The measurements given here make a petal measuring 6 x 6 inches (15 x 15 cm). You need four petals for a 12-inch (30-cm) block.

STEP 1

Draw an accurate 6-inch (15-cm) square.

STEP 2

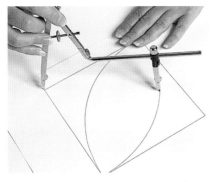

Place the compass point on one corner of the block and open the compass to exactly 6 inches (15 cm). Draw an arc from corner to corner. Then place the compass point on the opposite corner and draw another arc from corner to corner.

TO DRAFT ALABAMA BEAUTY

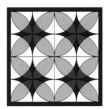

The measurements given here are for a 12 x 12-inch (30 x 30-cm) block.

STEP 1

Draw an accurate 12-inch (30-cm) square.

STEP 2

Place the compass point on one corner and open the compass to 6 inches (15 cm). Draw an arc from one side of the square to the other.

STEP 3

Repeat the same process for each of the other three corners.

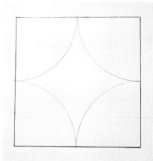

STEP 4

Draft the petals using the method described for Melon Patch petal.

TO DRAFT DRUNKARD'S PATH

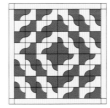

The measurements given here are for a 6 x 6-inch (15 x 15-cm) block.

STEP 1

Draw an accurate 6-inch (15-cm) square.

STEP 2

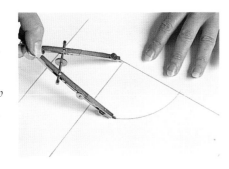

Place the compass point on the corner of the square and open the compass to 3 inches (7.5 cm). Draw an arc from one side of the square to the other.

STEP 3

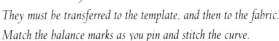

Mark the curves of the design at regular intervals. (These are known as balance marks.) They must be transferred to the template, and then to the fabric. Match the balance marks as you pin and stitch the curve.

MAKING THE QUILT TOP

Follow this procedure to construct quilt blocks. First, make a sketch of your block and color it in to indicate where the different colors and fabrics will go. Note how many shapes and patches you need of the different fabrics you've chosen.

PREPARING FABRICS

Some quilters like to wash their fabrics before use, usually when using dark colors that may bleed into lighter colors. Either way, iron the fabrics well before cutting. To give them a nice crisp finish and to make the cutting process easier, use spray starch before ironing.

CUTTING PATCHES USING SCISSORS

STEP 1

Lay each template on the fabric and draw around it using a soft (2B or #2) pencil.

STEP 2

Using sharp fabric scissors, cut the patch exactly on the line.

CUTTING PATCHES USING A ROTARY CUTTER AND MAT

The instructions here and throughout the book assume you're right-handed. Reverse them if you are left-handed.

If you're making a large project, such as a quilt with several repeated blocks, a rotary cutter and self-healing mat make things a lot quicker and easier. The blade of the cutter is extremely sharp, so you must follow some simple safety rules when using this equipment:

- **ALWAYS** *put on the lock, which all cutters have, at the end of each cut. If possible, buy a cutter with an automatic lock, which retracts the blade as soon as you stop cutting.*
- **ALWAYS** *run the blade away from you, never toward you.*
- **ALWAYS** *keep the cutter in a safe place, away from children.*

STEP 1

Iron the fabric well. You can cut several layers at a time if you make sure that the folds especially are well ironed. Place the fabric on the cutting mat with rough edges to your right. Place the ruler on the fabric, leaving the rough edge exposed. Press down firmly on the ruler with your left hand. Run the rotary blade along the edge of the ruler to trim off the right edge evenly.

A cutting mat, a rotary cutter, and a ruler are essential equipment for rotary cutting.

STEP 2

Turn the trimmed edge to your left, lay the ruler along the trimmed edge in line with the measurement you need, and cut along the edge of the ruler.

STEP 3

To make patches from the strips, line up as before with the markings on the ruler.

STEP 4

Make triangles by cutting diagonally across squares.

STITCHING

Patchwork can be sewn by hand or by machine, although there are obvious advantages to machine sewing when you're working on a large project.

HAND STITCHING

A straightforward running stitch is used, except for English patchwork (see page 26).

Use a fine, sharp needle and thread to match your fabric, or a neutral color if you are using a variety of fabric colors. Begin and end each seam exactly ¼ inch (6 mm) before the end; in other words, do *not* sew into the seam allowance. You may find it helpful at first to draw in the stitching line as a guide, marking a small dot where stitching begins and ends. Once you've made a few blocks using this method, you'll probably find that you can estimate the seam allowance accurately just by eye.

STEP 1

Take a small backstitch at the beginning and end of each seam and make evenly spaced running stitches along the seam allowance.

STEP 2

To join patches with matching seams, sew up to the marked dot and then pass the needle though to the next dot, without sewing into the seam allowances. This means that when you are ready to press the patchwork, you can press the seams in whichever direction you choose.

ENGLISH PATCHWORK

English patchwork, also known as mosaic patchwork, is a method of piecing patchwork over paper templates. The patches, which are made by basting fabric over the templates, are then hand stitched together by taking small stitches across the tops of the patches.

The advantage of this method of patchwork is that it makes it possible to handle fabrics like silk and satin because the papers anchor them while they are being sewn together. It also makes awkward angles easy, which is one reason for calling it "mosaic" patchwork—complicated geometric shapes can easily be fitted together just as in mosaic tiles. Last, but not least, it's easy to carry around and can be picked up and worked on in odd moments.

STEP 1

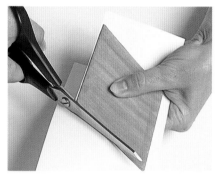

Draw around your master templates on paper and cut out as many paper templates as you will need for each shape. The total number will depend on your particular project. If you need a lot of paper templates, you can cut out several at a time. Layer three or four papers together under the template, hold them firmly in your left hand, and cut around the edge of the template.

STEP 2

Lay a paper template on a piece of fabric and pin it in place.

STEP 3

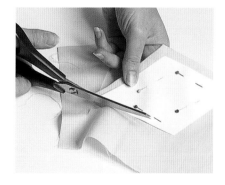

Cut out the fabric, leaving at least ¼ inch (6 mm) all around the template.

STEP 4

Fold the fabric allowance over each edge of the paper and baste all around, folding in the fabric at the corners. Secure the corners by taking a small backstitch each time you come to one.

STEP 5

Place the patches right sides together with the edges even. Make a knot in the thread and bring the thread through from the back so that

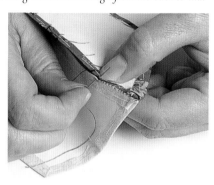

the knot is hidden in the turning. Topstitch the edges with small, neat stitches. Finish each seam by making a few backstitches and then snipping off the thread.

STEP 6

To fit a third patch into a tight angle, realign the patches and sew the first seam. Instead of continuing with the same thread, finish off each seam with a few backstitches, snip off the thread, and start each seam again. You'll get a stronger seam this way.

STEP 7

When the patchwork is complete, take out the basting stitches, remove the paper patches, and press gently. If you take out the papers carefully, you can reuse them.

MACHINE STITCHING

A straight running stitch is all that's required to join patches and blocks by machine.

STEP 1

Check that the tension on your machine is even, and set the stitch length to between 9 and 12 stitches to the inch (between 5 and 8 stitches per cm).

STEP 2

Lay the patches right sides together so that the edges are even. Stitch exactly ¼ inch (6 mm) in from the edge.

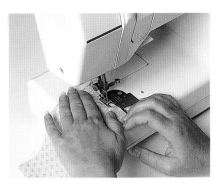

STEP 3

Press the seams. Machine-stitched seams can either be pressed to one side, as in hand piecing, or open.

SEAM ALLOWANCE

An accurate seam allowance is important because if it is uneven the units of the block won't meet up neatly and your blocks may be of uneven sizes. Of course, you may wish to mark the seam allowance on each patch, but that's laborious when making a large project. Two alternative ways of getting an accurate seam allowance are:

- *Use a special ¼-inch (6-mm) foot, if your machine has one.*
- *Mark the throat plate of your machine so that you can see where to sew. Place a ruler under the machine needle and lower the needle so that it rests exactly on the ¼-inch (6-mm) mark. With the ruler still in position, run a strip of masking tape alongside it. Place the edge of the fabric against the tape.*
- *You can buy a magnetic seam marker. This device is placed on the throat plate to guide the edge of the fabric. Please note that magnets should not be used with or near computerized machines.*

SETTING IN PATCHES

Some blocks involve awkward angles and can only be pieced by setting the patches into the angles. It sounds complicated, but setting in patches is easy if you remember *not* to sew into the seam allowance. You'll find it best to mark the end of the sewing line with a small dot.

STEP 1

Place the first two patches right sides together and sew the seam between the marked dots. At the beginning and end, anchor the thread with a small backstitch.

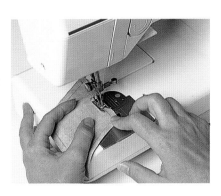

STEP 2

Position the third patch and, again, stitch exactly to the dot. Pivot the work so that the final seam lines up with the first two and sew from dot to dot.

STEP 3

Gently press the completed block, first from the back and then from the front.

SEWING CURVES

Curved seams need care but can easily be mastered using the following method:

STEP 1

Make regular marks (balance marks) on the curves in the drafted pattern.

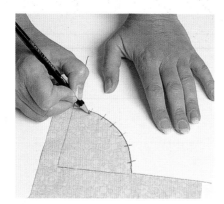

STEP 2

Transfer the marks on the templates to the fabric patches and match them as you ease the curve into position and pin it.

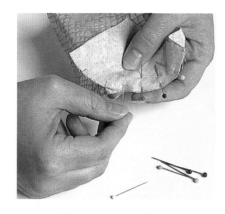

STEP 3

When you have finished stitching, snip tiny notches at the convex (outward) curves to make them lie flat. These should be not quite as deep as the seam allowance.

STEP 4

Press the seam gently from the back, then on the front.

MAKING A BLOCK

Begin by laying out the patches as they appear in the block. Always try to arrange them so that they can be joined in straight rows, but if some of the shapes need set-in seams, follow the instructions on page 27 for doing this.

STEP 1

Join patches by placing two right sides together, pinning them together, and stitching exactly ¼ inch (6 mm) from the edge.

STEP 2

Join each unit to the next one to form a row of patches.

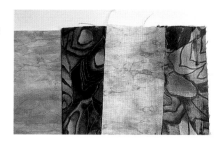

STEP 3

Join the rows. Where seams meet, if they are pressed open, match and pin the two seams evenly. If the seams are pressed to one side, finger press them in opposite directions before pinning.

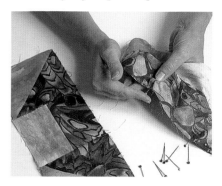

STEP 4

Press the completed block carefully from the back, taking care not to stretch the fabrics. Lift and replace the iron rather than pushing it over the surface.

STEP 5

Turn to the front and press again.

FOUNDATION PIECING

Foundation piecing is a useful technique for constructing blocks that require intricate piecing. It's particularly good for Log Cabin, where the number of strips involved can often result in inaccurate measurements in the finished blocks. This is the method recommended for making the Twisted Log Cabin quilts. You can work either on a very thin fabric foundation, such as fine muslin (in which case the foundation is left in the blocks as described above), or on ordinary paper that you will tear off when the block is finished. There are also specialty craft papers sold for this purpose.

Mark the pattern of the block on one side of the foundation fabric. If you want to make several blocks, you can make copies on a photocopier or print them from a quilting program on your computer, if you have one. Another method is to draw the pattern on one piece of paper, place several layers of paper under the top one, and pin them together. Remove the thread from both the bobbin and the spool on your sewing machine and stitch over the pattern through all the layers. The needle marks will make a clear and accurate line for you to follow.

If you are using a paper foundation that is to be pulled off on completion, set your machine stitch shorter than usual—say, 9 stitches to the inch (5 stitches per cm). Always take two or three stitches beyond the marked sewing line to secure it.

FOUNDATION PIECING FOR LOG CABIN BLOCKS

Work from the center of the block outward. Measure and cut each strip as you place it for stitching. Many other blocks can be constructed in this way; however, where lots of different shapes are required, the patches must be stitched in the correct order, so this must be marked on the

pattern. Lots of ready-to-use foundation patterns are now available to buy, and computer quilting programs usually contain an extensive selection of them.

STEP 1

Place the center square right side up on the unmarked side of the paper, making sure that it completely covers the stitching line. (Hold it up to the light to check.) Then pin it in place.

STEP 2

Take the first strip and place it on top of the center patch, right sides together. Check that when the strip is pressed open it will cover the next stitching line. Pin it in place.

STEP 3

Turn the foundation paper over so that you can see the marked pattern and stitch along the marked line. Turn back to the right side and press the strip open.

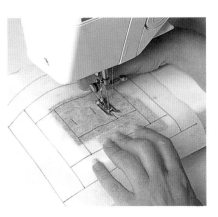

STEP 4

Repeat this process until all the strips have been added. Now remove the papers, taking care not to pull too roughly on the stitches.

SETTINGS AND LAYOUTS

Although some of the quilts in this book depend for their illusionary effect on placing repeated blocks side by side, others need to be set with sashings—vertical and horizontal strips between blocks—to achieve their effect. Some need to be set on point, or diagonally.

SETTING BLOCKS WITH PLAIN SASHINGS

Sashings can either be plain (of a single fabric) or have squares in a contrasting fabric, known as posts, where the strips meet. To add sashings, you need extra fabric that complements the blocks in the quilt top. Remember to add a ¼-inch (6-mm) seam allowance to all your measurements when cutting sashing strips.

FOR PLAIN SASHINGS

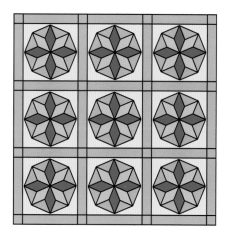

STEP 1

First decide on the width of the sashings, which should be in proportion to the size of the blocks. For example, a 3-inch (7.5-cm) sashing looks to scale on a standard 12-inch (30-cm) block. Each row of blocks is joined by strips the same length as the blocks. For example, use strips 12 inches (30 cm) long to join 12-inch (30-cm) blocks. Remember that the unfinished blocks will measure 12½ inches (31 cm), including the seam allowance, so that's the length you'll need to cut the sashing strips.

STEP 2

Work out how many sashing strips you need and cut that number. For example, to join three blocks you will need two strips plus one each for the beginning and end of the row, plus two strips for the top and bottom.

STEP 3

Place a sashing strip on the first block with right sides together, pin, and stitch.

STEP 4

Place the next sashing strip on the other side of the block, pin, and stitch. Continue in this way until all the rows of blocks have been joined. Press all seams away from the sashing.

STEP 5

Work out how many long sashing strips you will need. (This will depend on how many rows of blocks there are.) Measure the rows and cut strips to this length. You will need two additional strips—one for the top and one for the bottom.

FOR SASHINGS WITH POSTS

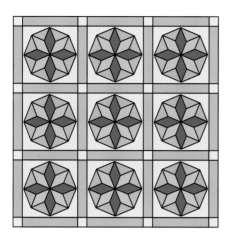

STEP 1

Count the number of joining strips needed, including strips for the top and bottom of the quilt, in the same way as for plain sashings. Join the blocks in rows with sashing strips, adding one at each end of the row.

STEP 2

Cut squares exactly the same size as the width of the sashing strips.

STEP 3

Make horizontal strips by joining squares and sashing strips, beginning and ending each row with a square. Join rows of blocks with strips, taking care to match the seams where the sashings meet. Finally, add a row of sashing strips and squares, one to the top and one to the bottom.

SETTING BLOCKS "ON POINT"

The blocks are set diagonally across the quilt in rows. Half-blocks or triangles must be added to complete the rows.

The fan blocks in this quilt are set "on point."

BORDERS

Not every quilt needs borders, but borders can often set off the blocks and considerably enhance the quilt top. There are several types of borders: Plain strips can be added to the top, bottom, and sides, or the strips can be finished with square posts at the corners. Alternatively, the corners can be mitered with a diagonal seam at each corner, like a picture frame. This useful technique is also used in the construction of some blocks, such as Attic Windows.

Borders and edge finishes play an important part in the overall visual impact of a quilt.

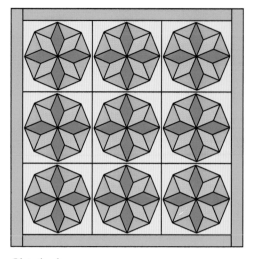

Plain borders

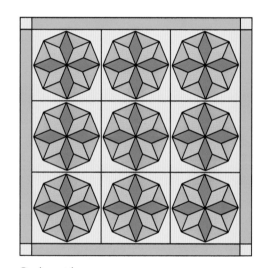

Borders with corner posts

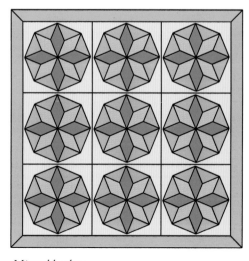

Mitered borders

TO MITER CORNERS ON BORDERS

Mitering corners needs a little practice, but the effect is well worth the effort. The secret is *not* to stitch into the seam allowances at the corners.

STEP 1

Decide on the width of your border and add the seam allowance.

STEP 2

Measure the length and width of the quilt top.

STEP 3

Cut strips to those measurements plus twice the width of the border, including seam allowances. For example, if the quilt top measures 48 x 48 inches (122 x 122 cm) and the border is 3 inches (9 cm) wide, cut border strips 55 inches (142 cm) long.

STEP 4

Pin and stitch borders to the edge of the quilt on all four sides, leaving an equal amount of extra fabric at each end.

STEP 5

Stitch, taking a ¼-inch (6-mm) seam allowance, but begin and end the seam exactly ¼ inch (6 mm) from each end. Backstitch at each end of the line of sewing.

STEP 6

Press the borders open and lay out the quilt top on a flat surface. Let the extensions overlap each other and turn under the top one at an angle of 45 degrees. Pin and slipstitch the top strip to the bottom. Press well.

STEP 7

Turn to the back and trim away excess. Press the seam again.

ADDING BORDERS TO ENGLISH PATCHWORK

A different technique is needed for adding borders to English patchwork.

STEP 1

When you have removed the backing papers, leave the edges of the patches turned under and press them neatly.

STEP 2

Cut border strips to the width and length required.

STEP 3

With right sides together, pin the border strips to the patchwork with the raw edge of the border strip even with the folded edge of the patchwork.

STEP 4

Stitch, taking a narrow seam and stitching as close as possible to the junctions of the patches. Open the borders and press.

QUILTING AND FINISHING

When you have completed the quilt top and added any borders, the next stage is to prepare it for quilting and finishing. For this, you need a large flat surface on which to lay out the quilt. A large table is ideal, but if you don't have one, use the floor. If a quilting pattern is to be marked on the top, it must be done at this stage.

STENCILING PATTERNS

Patterns can be either stenciled on or traced from patterns.

STEP 1

Draw the pattern in black pen on good-quality drawing paper and fix it to a table or other flat surface with masking tape.

STEP 2

Place the quilt top over the pattern and anchor it with masking tape.

STEP 3

Trace or stencil the quilting pattern onto the quilt top, using either a soft pencil or a marker that can easily be removed after quilting. White quilt-marking pencils are good for marking dark fabrics.

STEP 4

If the pattern doesn't show through (for example, under a dark fabric), fix the pattern to a window with masking tape and fix the top over it. Alternatively, use a light box. You can improvise one by supporting a sheet of glass on piles of books and placing a lamp under it.

If the quilt is to be set into a floor frame for quilting, no basting is needed. Otherwise, proceed as follows.

BASTING THE QUILT "SANDWICH"

STEP 1

Measure the quilt top and cut both backing and batting at least 2 inches (5 cm) larger all around. If you are intending to use the

self-binding method (see page 39), you must leave a sufficient extra allowance on the backing to turn it over to the front. Press the backing well and lay it out on the surface, right side down. Lay the batting on top of it and smooth it out carefully.

STEP 2

Lay the quilt top on top of the batting, right side up, and use long, glass-headed pins to pin it all over at regular intervals.

STEP 3

Using a large needle and a long thread, baste through all three layers. Take big stitches and either work in a grid, first across and then from top to bottom, or work outward diagonally from the center. Now the quilt is ready for quilting.

QUILTING

There are several quilting options. Patterns can be used, as described above, or you can quilt a regular ¼ inch (6 mm) inside each patch—a method known as outline quilting. The quilt can also be finished by tying it at regular intervals with perle cotton or knitting wool. For regular quilting, the choice is between hand or machine quilting.

HAND QUILTING

The three layers of the quilt need to be kept under tension to prevent them from slipping apart. Most quilts can easily be quilted in a hoop. For really large ones, floor frames are available, but they need a lot of space, which may not be convenient if the quilting is going to take some time. The advantage of using a floor frame is that you do not need to baste the quilt before you place it in the frame.

A good alternative is to use one of the extra-large hoops that are designed for this purpose. Place the hoop over one section of the quilt; when you have finished quilting that section, move the hoop to the next section. Continue like this until the quilting is complete.

In order to quilt right up to the edges of the quilt, baste strips of plain fabric to the edges so that the hoop can extend over the area to be quilted.

The hand-quilting stitch is a simple running stitch. Note that the stitches must go through all three layers of the quilt and must be as even as possible. Evenness is more important than the size of the stitches.

STEP 1

Wear a thimble on the second finger of your right hand. A thimble with a small ridge around the crown is best. Using a quilting needle (known as a "between") and quilting thread, make a knot in the thread. Bring the thread up from the back of the quilt to the surface, gently pulling the knot into the batting. Take a small backstitch.

STEP 2

Begin quilting by pushing the needle through all three layers, keeping the needle as straight as possible. Keep your left hand under the place where you're working and use your finger to gently push the fabric up just in front of the needle. You should feel the point of the needle at each stitch. You may want to use a finger guard if your finger becomes sore.

STEP 3

Take several stitches before pulling the thread through. Aim for a light rocking motion with the needle. This is best achieved by lodging the needle against the rim of the thimble.

STEP 4

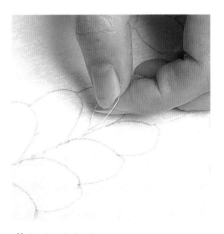

At the end of the thread, make a knot in it and take a small backstitch. Push the needle into the batting and bring it out a short distance away. Pull the thread gently until the knot pops into the backing. Snip off the thread closely.

MACHINE QUILTING

Machine quilting makes the task much quicker than hand quilting; but it's advisable to practice the techniques before you embark on a large project.

There are two basic types of machine quilting: straight machine quilting, for any patterns that can be stitched in straight lines or gentle curves, and free machine quilting for patterns with more exaggerated curves.

STRAIGHT MACHINE QUILTING

STEP 1

Before you begin, make a practice piece. Attach an even-feed foot or walking foot. Use no. 80 machine needles and good-quality machine thread.

STEP 2

Check that the tension is correct (check back and front) and that the fabric isn't puckering up. Quilt across the first lines to make squares and, again, check for puckering and dragging. Adjust the tension and stitch length until you're happy with the result.

STEP 3

Place the portion of the quilt to be quilted under the needle. If necessary, roll up one section of the quilt and secure it with clips.

STEP 4

Place your hands on either side of the portion to be quilted and press down gently but firmly. Soft cotton gardening gloves with small rubber grippers make it easy to hold on to the quilt as you work.

STEP 5

Start and end each row with a couple of backstitches. When stitching is complete, thread the ends through a needle, draw them through the fabric layers, and bring them up at the back of the quilt. Tie off and snip.

FREE MACHINE QUILTING

Quilting patterns can be either marked on the quilt surface or drawn on tracing paper that is pinned to the surface and torn away when quilting is finished.

STEP 1

For free machine quilting, either drop the feed dog or cover it with a special plate, depending on your machine.

STEP 2

Fit a darning foot, or a special quilting foot if your machine has one. Set the needle length to 0 and lower the tension slightly. Make some samples as described for straight machine stitching. (This is particularly important for free machine stitching, as learning to control the speed and movement of the work requires practice.)

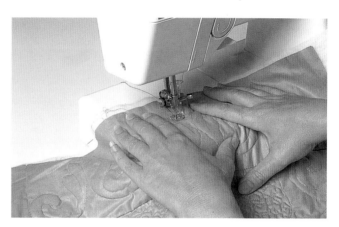

STEP 3

Begin by taking a single stitch, turning the wheel manually, then bring the thread from the bobbin up to the top. This will ensure it doesn't snarl up as you begin stitching.

This stippling pattern is stitched using the free machine method.

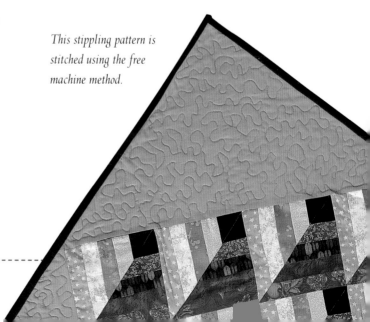

STEP 4

Running the machine at a slightly slower rate than for ordinary sewing, begin sewing. Because the feed dog is disconnected, you must manually move the quilt under the needle. Move it as evenly and steadily as possible. If you move it too fast, the stitches will be too large; too slowly, the stitches will be too small. Instead of marking the quilting design directly onto the quilt, try drawing it on tracing paper, pinning the tracing paper to the quilt top, and stitching through the paper. Tear away the paper when you have finished quilting.

STEP 5

Meander, or stippling quilting is done by moving the quilt under the needle to make random patterns. This needs some practice but is such a useful technique that it's well worth spending some time to grasp it.

TYING A QUILT

This is a quick and easy way of anchoring the layers of a quilt.

STEP 1

Use a long needle and strong thread, such as coton à broder or embroidery silk.

STEP 2

Pass the needle through all three layers, leaving a tail of about 2 inches (5 cm) on the top. Bring the needle back to the top very close to where it went in.

STEP 3

Take another stitch like this and snip off, again leaving a tail.

STEP 4

Tie the ends together in a knot and snip off the ends to about 1 inch (2.5 cm) or less.

FINISHING THE QUILT

When you have completed the quilting and removed the basting stitches, finish the edges by binding them or by turning them in—a technique known as butting. Alternatively, the backing can be folded over to the front, turned under, and hemmed down. Of course, this option is only possible if you've left sufficient excess of backing on all sides.

BINDING EDGES

In this method, separate strips of fabric make the binding.

STEP 1

Measure the width of the quilt and cut 3-inch (7.5-cm) wide strips to that length.

STEP 2

Fold each strip in half lengthwise, wrong sides together, and press.

STEP 3

With right sides together and lining up the raw edges, pin and stitch the strips to the top and bottom of the quilt.

STEP 4

Turn the strips to the back and hem them down.

STEP 5

Measure the length of the quilt and cut 3-inch (7.5-cm) wide strips to that length, adding enough extra length to turn under at the ends. Fold in half lengthwise and press. Pin and stitch the strips to the sides of the quilt, turn to the back, and hem them down, turning in the ends of the strips.

BUTTING EDGES

In this method, the edges of the quilt top and backing are butted together so that there is no separate binding.

STEP 1

Turn the quilt top over the batting by at least ¼ inch (6 mm) and baste it in place.

STEP 2

Turn in the backing on to the quilt top with the raw edge folded under. Baste again.

STEP 3

Finish by slip-stitching the two edges together.

SELF-BINDING

In this method, the backing is folded over to the front of the quilt to form a binding. This provides visual continuity between the back and front of the quilt and is an easy way to finish the edges, provided you've left sufficient extra backing fabric to bring it over to the front of the quilt.

STEP 1

Trim off the excess batting so that it is level with the quilt top.

STEP 2

Fold the backing fabric so that the raw edge is level with the quilt top.

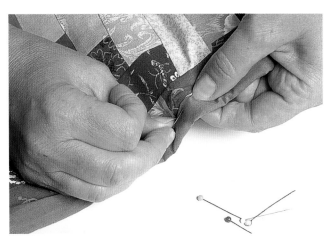

STEP 3

Fold the backing fabric again, then pin it to the front of the quilt.

STEP 4

Baste into position.

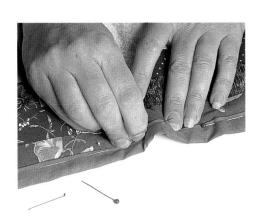

STEP 5

Hem to the front with invisible stitches.

ATTACHING A HANGING SLEEVE

In order to hang your quilt, whether as a wall hanging or at an exhibition or show, you must attach a hanging sleeve to it on the reverse near the top.

STEP 1

Measure the width of the quilt and cut a 6½-inch (16.5-cm) strip to that length.

STEP 2

Fold the strip in half lengthwise and press. Stitch along the long raw edge, taking a ¼-inch (6-mm) seam.

STEP 3

Refold the strip so that the seam is in the center and press the seam open.

STEP 4

Turn in and stitch the ends neatly.

STEP 5

Attach the sleeve to the top of the reverse of the quilt, with the seam underneath, and slipstitch into position. Pass a wooden batten or dowel through the sleeve to hang the quilt.

LABELING QUILTS

Relatively few nineteenth- and early twentieth-century quilts are labeled, yet how often do we look at an old quilt and wish that we knew the story behind it? Who made it? Where, when, and why? Make life easy for future generations by labeling your quilt. Label it with your name, the date, and any other useful information, such as who it was made for and why. Labels can be either written with special Pigma ink pens, which are resistant to light and water (colorfast), or embroidered. Embroidering is the most durable method.

BLUE STAR CROSS
CELIA EDDY
MARYPORT CUMBRIA
2003

Labeling your quilt will help future generations to identify your work.

SHORT CUTS

Here are some invaluable short cuts that will speed up your work considerably.

CUTTING PATCHES USING A ROTARY CUTTER

You can use a rotary cutter and mat to cut patches without going to the trouble of making templates. It's easy to cut regular shapes, like squares, rectangles, and triangles, like this, using the drafted block for the measurements. All measurements must have ¼ inch (6 mm) added on all sides for a seam allowance.

CUTTING SQUARES AND RECTANGLES

Measure one side of the shape and cut strips to that width. Cut the strips again to make squares or rectangles as required.

CUTTING OTHER SHAPES

You can also speed up the cutting of other shapes, but for these you will need to use a template. Measure the width of the shape and cut strips to that width. Lay the template on the strip and either mark it with a pencil or run the cutter along the edge of the template.

CUTTING HALF-SQUARE TRIANGLES

You can cut squares and then cut them in half diagonally, but you must measure the sides of the triangle first, including a seam allowance. Cut strips of that width, and then squares. Cut the squares in half diagonally.

CHAIN PIECING

Chain piecing is a quick way of sewing sets of identical patches. It saves thread, too.

STEP 1
Place a pile of pairs of patches, right sides together, beside the sewing machine.

STEP 2
Stitch the first pair along the seam line. At the end of the seam, do not snip the thread but take another couple of stitches beyond the fabric.

STEP 3
Feed in the next pair of patches.

STEP 4
Continue like this until all patches have been sewn, then snip the threads and press them as usual.

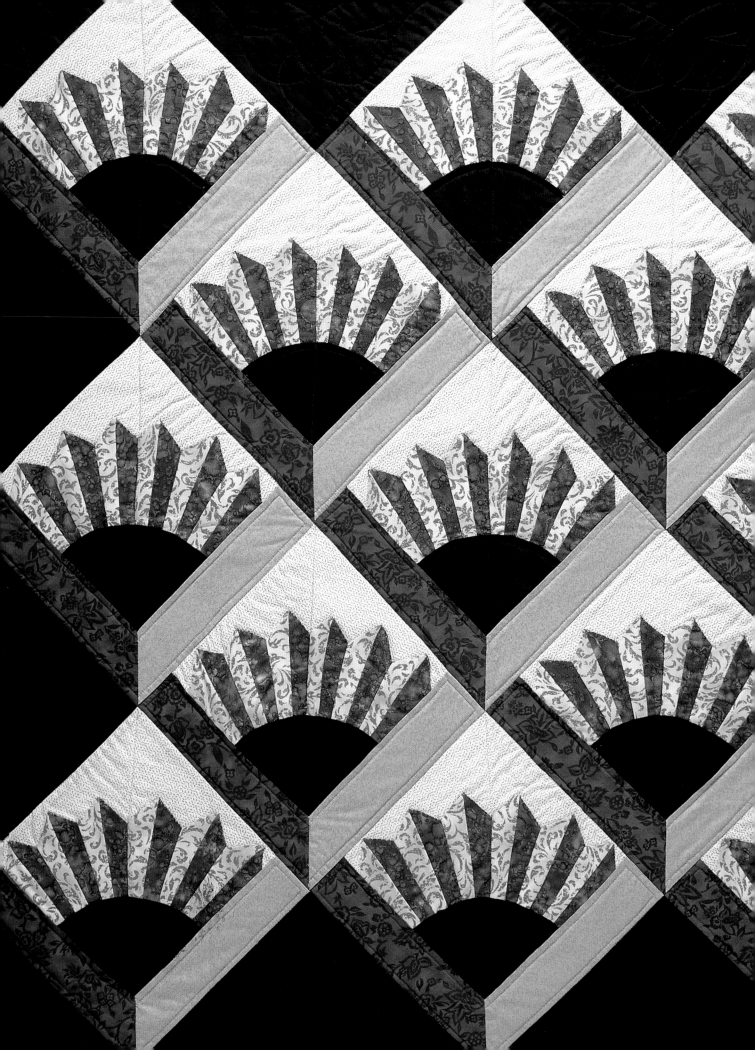

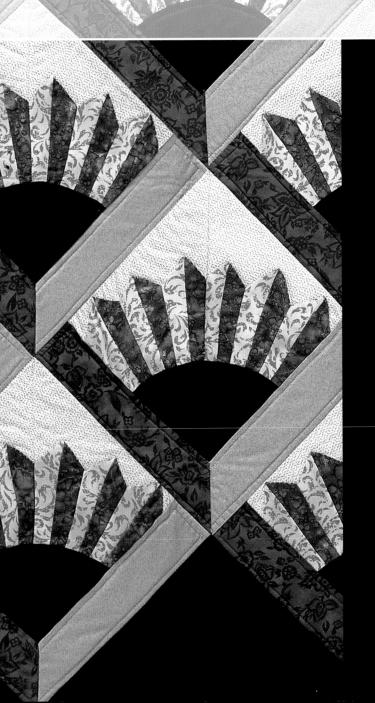

3D AND PERSPECTIVE

The illusion that a surface that we know to be two-dimensional LOOKS three-dimensional produces some of the most intriguing and satisfying effects in quilt making; the eye is fooled into seeing depth, perspective, and shadows, producing exciting and complex effects that, quite literally, lift the quilt surface into another dimension. How does this happen? We'll explain some simple rules for creating these illusions by the manipulation of certain shapes and colors within traditional patchwork patterns so that you can easily reproduce them yourself.

TUMBLING BLOCKS

Three-dimensional patterns are often drafted on an isometric grid (see Drafting and Design on page 21). Tumbling Blocks, Tumbling Blocks and Stars, and Right-Angle Patchwork are all examples of quilts designed like this.

Tumbling Blocks has long been a favorite with quilters. The Tumbling Block, or Baby Block, pattern appears as a floor and wall decoration in many ancient buildings, including the churches and palaces of Venice, which are a particularly rich source of geometric and mosaic patterns.

The impression of solid faceted blocks is created by joining three 60-degree diamonds in three colors or tones: dark, medium, and light.

Piece this pattern by hand, using the English patchwork method shown on page 26.

Only one template, drafted on an isometric grid, as shown below, is required.

FABRICS

You will need three fabrics for this design—one dark, one medium, and one light. You must make sure that the contrasts between the three tones are strong enough to emphasize the faceted effect. This is a classic pattern for a scrap quilt.

MAKING THE QUILT

STEP 1:

Following the instructions on page 21, draft the template and copy it onto template plastic or cardboard. Cut it out without adding a seam allowance. Using the English patchwork method (see page 26), cut the required number of papers from the template.

STEP 2:

Pin the papers to the wrong side of each fabric and cut out the patches, adding a generous ¼-inch (6-mm) seam allowance all around. For each block, cut one dark, one medium, and one light diamond.

STEP 3:

Fold the fabric over the paper and baste it onto the paper. Join the patches by placing them right sides

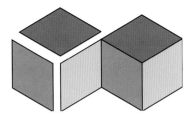

together and overstitching the joined edges (see English patchwork, page 26). Make up the blocks using the fabrics in the same position in each one.

STEP 4:

Join the blocks in rows.

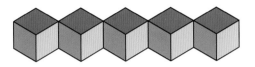

STEP 5:

Join the rows.

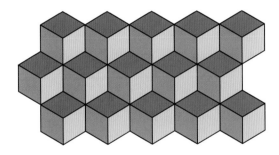

STEP 6:

When you have the required number of rows, finish with a row of diamond patches. Take out the basting stitches and remove the

papers. Press the patchwork gently but firmly on the front. Leave the turnings on the outside patches turned under.

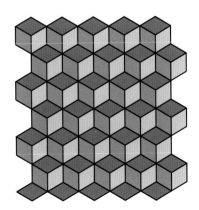

STEP 7:

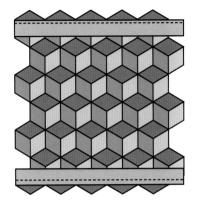

Following the instructions for adding borders to English patchwork on page 33, pin border strips, with the right sides together, to the top and bottom of the patchwork. Leave half-diamonds showing

at the top and bottom edges. Stitch the borders to the patchwork, taking a ¼-inch (6-mm) seam allowance on the border strip but stitching as close as possible to the junctions of the patches.

STEP 8:

Trim off the half-diamonds and press the borders open. Add border strips to the sides to cover the excess material, then stitch as above.

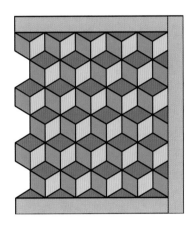

Completed Tumbling Blocks quilt top with plain borders.

45

TUMBLING BLOCKS AND STARS

In this arresting variation on the Tumbling Blocks theme, sets of seven cubes are grouped to form hexagons. These, in turn, are joined to black triangles to create the illusion that the blocks are floating on a dark background. The spaces between the blocks form stars, making up the pattern of Tumbling Blocks and Stars. To get the most striking effect, use the light, medium, and dark fabrics in the same position in each block. This will give the impression of a light source falling from one direction, lighting up the quilt surface.

The easiest way to construct this pattern is to use the English patchwork method, described on page 26. Follow the diagrams for the order of piecing. To complete the quilt, add a narrow border, using the same fabric that you used for the triangles to enhance the impression that the cubes are floating in space.

FABRICS

You will need light, medium, and dark tones of each of seven different colors, plus black for the background and border.

MAKING THE QUILT

STEP 1:

Following the instructions on page 21, draft templates Templates A, B, and C on an isometric grid and copy them onto template plastic or cardboard. Cut out without adding a seam allowance.

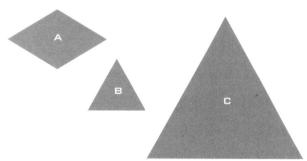

STEP 2:

Following the instructions for English patchwork on page 26, use these templates to cut the required number of papers, without adding a seam allowance.

STEP 3:

Using your first color group, pin the papers cut from Template A to the wrong side of the fabrics and cut out seven patches from each one, adding a ¼-inch (6-mm) seam allowance all around.

STEP 4:

Fold the fabric over the papers and baste. Join the patches by placing them right sides together and overstitching. Piece seven cubes as shown below.

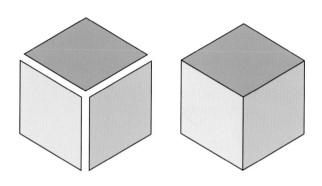

STEP 5:

Using Template B, cut twelve small black triangles, adding a ¼-inch (6-mm) seam allowance all around, and baste them to the paper templates. Working from the center outward, join each set of seven cubes into a large hexagon.

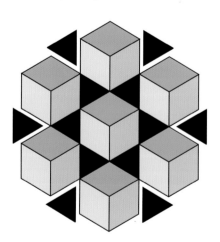

46

STEP 6:

Make six more hexagons in the same way, each one in a different color group.

STEP 7:

Using Template C, cut twelve large black triangles, adding a ¼-inch (6-mm) seam allowance all around, and baste them to the paper templates. Working from the center outward, join the seven hexagons together.

STEP 8:

When the patchwork is complete, take out the basting stitches and remove the papers.

STEP 9:

Measure the sides of the quilt and make mitered borders as shown on page 33. Add the borders, following the instructions for adding borders to English patchwork, also on page 33. Finish the edges by binding or butting, as shown on page 38.

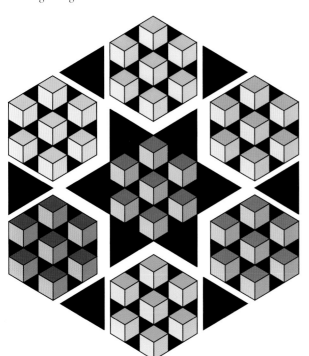

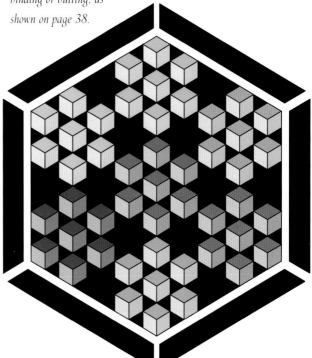

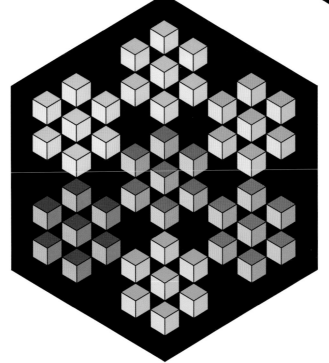

Completed Tumbling Blocks and Stars Quilt. Adding black borders enhances the effect of floating blocks.

Only one template is needed—a half-hexagon. Draft this template, as shown below, on an isometric grid.

Each block consists of three hexagons, each one pieced in two halves. The illusory effect of stacked boxes is achieved by the color placement. Once again, this pattern is best pieced over papers, using the English patchwork method described on page 26, and is ideal for a scrap quilt.

FABRICS
As with Tumbling Blocks, this pattern is achieved by using three fabrics—light, medium, and dark. Scrap fabrics are fine, provided you choose fabrics within the light, medium, and dark ranges.

MAKING THE QUILT
STEP 1:
Following the instructions on page 21, draft the template and copy it onto template plastic or cardboard. Cut out the template without adding a seam allowance. Using the English patchwork method (see page 26), cut the required number of papers.

STEP 2:
Pin the papers to the wrong side of the fabric and cut out the patches, leaving a ¼-inch (6-mm) seam allowance all around. Cut two light, two medium, and two dark half-hexagons for each block. Fold the fabric over the papers and baste.

RIGHT-ANGLE PATCHWORK

Drafted on an isometric grid and using dark, medium, and light tones to produce the illusion of stacked boxes, Right-Angle Patchwork works on the same principle as Tumbling Blocks. The pattern has been in circulation since at least 1882, when it was published under the name Ecclesiastical. Another traditional name for it is Trefoil. Jinny Beyer called it Inner City, since the stacked blocks can suggest the shapes of high-rise buildings.

STEP 3:

Make three whole hexagons by joining a dark to a light, a dark to a medium, and a light to a medium half-hexagon. Join each pair of half-hexagons by placing the patches right sides together and overstitching.

STEP 4:

Join the three hexagons in the same way to make the block.

STEP 5:

Join blocks together to build up the patchwork to the required size. Fill in any gaps, at the top and bottom of the quilt, with two-patch hexagons

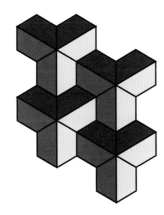

STEP 6:

Take out the basting stitches and remove the papers. Press the patchwork gently but firmly on the front. Leave the turnings on the outside patches turned under.

STEP 7:

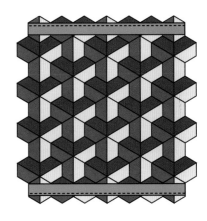

Following the instructions for adding borders to English patchwork on page 33, pin border strips, with the right sides together, to the top and bottom of the patchwork, leaving half-patches showing at the edges. Stitch the borders to the patchwork, taking a ¼-inch (6-mm) seam allowance on the border strip but stitching as close as possible to the junction of the patches.

STEP 8:

Trim off the half-patches and press the border open. Repeat the process to add border strips to the sides.

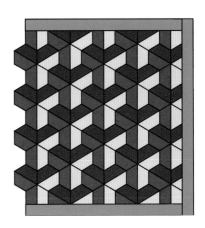

Completed Right-Angle Patchwork quilt top with plain borders.

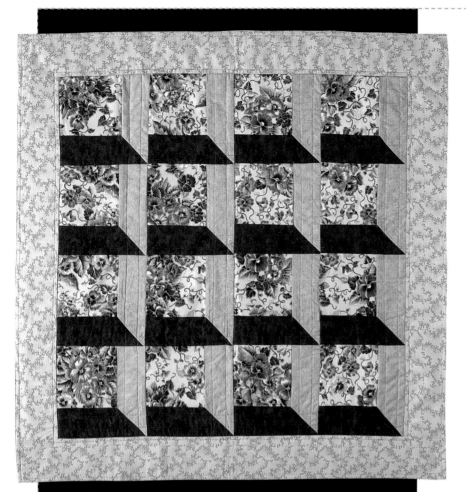

The success of this design depends on a strong contrast between the two patches that form the frames. Striped fabric can be used to emphasize the horizontal or vertical planes of the pattern. The 3D effect is partly a result of the mitering of the corners where these planes meet.

Only two templates are needed—Template A for the center of the window and Template B, which is reversed to make the patches for the frame of each window. Draft templates on a 12 x 12 square grid as shown below.

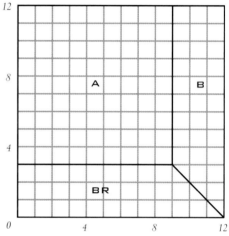

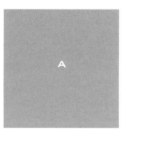

FABRICS

You will need three fabrics for this design—a strongly patterned or bright fabric for the center of the window (Fabric 1), and two others that complement Fabric 1 and contrast well with each other (Fabrics 2 and 3).

ATTIC WINDOWS

Attic Windows is another optical illusion pattern that is often seen in ancient floor tiles and wall decorations. It has been published as a patchwork pattern since the mid-nineteenth century and is a firm favorite with quilt makers today. It is simple to construct yet offers infinite design possibilities. You can look through the frames of your windows onto any scene. The sky, weather, gardens, and landscapes are all popular themes, but the outlook can just as easily be an abstract design.

MAKING THE QUILT

STEP 1:

Following the instructions on page 21, make Templates A and B, adding a ¼-inch (6-mm) seam allowance all around.

STEP 2:

Using Template A, cut the required number of patches from Fabric 1.

STEP 3:

Using Template B, cut the same number of patches from Fabric 2.

STEP 4:

Reverse Template B and cut the same number of patches from Fabric 3.

STEP 5:

To make each block, join one Template B frame patch to the right-hand side of the center square, right sides together, stitching up to, but not into, the seam allowance.

STEP 6:

Join the Template BR frame patch to the base of the center patch, again stitching up to but not into the seam allowance.

STEP 7:

Finish the corner by joining the two frame patches. (See page 33 for instructions on mitering.)

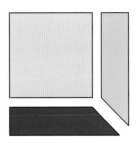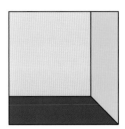

STEP 8:

Join the blocks in rows and add plain borders, as shown on page 32.

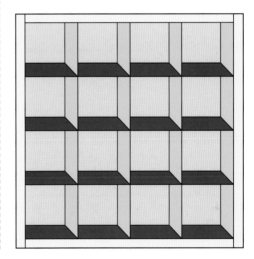

Completed Attic Windows quilt top with plain borders.

ATTIC WINDOWS VARIATIONS

Using the method shown above, you can create variations on the basic design. The "windows" can be elongated or stretched, and the "frames" can be made wider or thinner to suit the design.

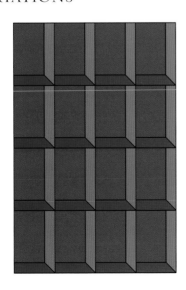

The blocks can be made taller by drafting the pattern on a grid that is longer than it is wide.

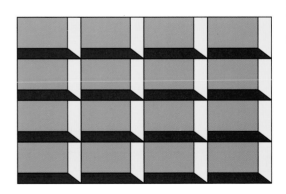

In this variation the windows are stretched, making the grid wider than it is long.

DEEP BOXES

This variation on the Attic Windows theme illustrates the versatility of this pattern. The depth of the frames has been increased. When you rotate the joined blocks, you create the illusion of deep boxes.

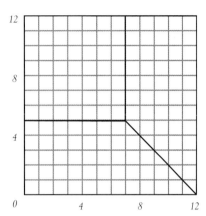

FABRICS

You will need four fabrics for this variation—a dark fabric for the center of the window (Fabric 1), two others that complement Fabric 1 and contrast well with each other (Fabrics 2 and 3), and a fabric that complements all three fabrics, for the four corner triangles (Fabric 4).

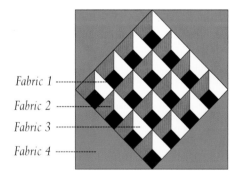

Fabric 1 ----------
Fabric 2 ----------
Fabric 3 ----------
Fabric 4 ----------

MAKING THE QUILT

STEP 1:

Draft the block on a square grid, as for other Attic Windows blocks, but increase the width of the frames relative to the center square. For example, give a 4-inch (10-cm) square a 3-inch (7.5-cm) frame.

STEP 2:

Choose a very dark fabric for the center square; black is a most effective choice for creating the impression of depth.

STEP 3:

Choose two colors, or strongly contrasting shades of one color, for the frames.

STEP 4:

Cut and piece the blocks, following the instructions for the basic Attic Windows pattern on page 51.

STEP 5:

Join the pieced squares in rows, then turn the completed piece to make a square "on point."

STEP 6:

To add the triangles to the sides, measure the side of the pieced quilt top. Cut a square piece of Fabric 4 to that measurement, adding a ¼-inch (6-mm) seam allowance all round. Cut the fabric in half diagonally to make two right triangles, then cut the triangles in half, to make four triangles. Add one triangle to each side of the pieced top.

Completed Deep Boxes quilt, showing rotated pieced boxes with triangles added to complete the quilt top.

BOXES VARIATION

Many blocks look effective in this setting. This is Compass Cross.

When two-colored Attic Windows-style frames are added to two sides, and the blocks are set on point, they appear to be boxes.

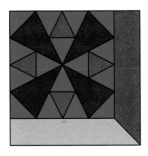

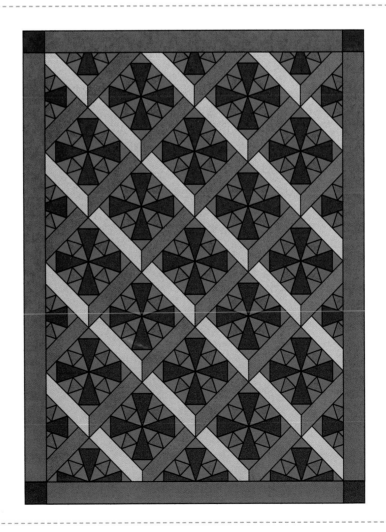

Only one template is needed—a right triangle. The size of the triangle depends on the finished depth of the bands (see Step 5).

FABRICS

The sides of the box are made using the strip-piecing method, shown below, to make two bands of fabric—one in light fabrics (Band A), and one in dark fabrics (Band B). The light and dark strips must all be the same width, but you can choose any width you like. You can use as many fabrics as you like, but the bottom band of each strip should be the same color (black in this quilt), and twice the width of the other strips.

SCRAP BOXES

Scrap Boxes uses many different fabrics to create a striking variation on the Attic Windows theme. The design is unified by using a single dark fabric for the bottom of the boxes. By carefully orchestrating dark and light tones in the strips on the two sides of the box, you can reinforce the impression of depth.

MAKING THE QUILT

STEP 1:

Select light fabrics for Band A. Select the same number of dark fabrics for Band B.

STEP 2:

Cut the strips to the desired width, adding a ½-inch (1-cm) seam allowance. For example, if you want the finished width of each strip to be 2 inches (5 cm), cut them to 2½ inches (6 cm). Cut all the strips to the same length.

STEP 3:

Cut strips of black fabric to twice the width of the colored strips plus a ½-inch (1-cm) seam allowance. For example, if the colored strips will be 2 inches (5 cm) when pieced, cut black fabric 4½ inches (12 cm) wide to give a finished size of 4 inches (10 cm).

STEP 4:

Join the strips to make two bands.

Band A

Band B

STEP 5:

Measure the depth of the bands to determine the size of the triangle template. For example, if the bands are 12 inches (30 cm) deep, draft a square of that measurement and cut it in half diagonally. Make the template following the instructions on page 21.

STEP 6:

Using the template, cut triangles from Band A:

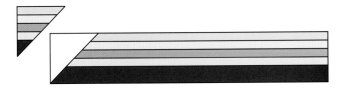

STEP 7:

Reverse the template and cut the same number of shapes from Band B:

STEP 8:

Join one dark and one light triangle along their long sides to form a square.

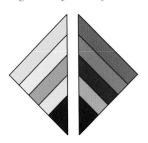

STEP 9:

Join the pieced squares in rows, and turn the completed piece to make a square "on point."

STEP 10:

Complete the quilt by setting triangles at the corners, following the instructions for Deep Boxes on page 52. Finish by binding or butting the edges, as shown on page 38.

Completed Scrap Boxes quilt top.

Three templates are needed for this block. Enlarge the drafted block below by 400 percent and follow the instructions to make a 10-inch (25-cm) block.

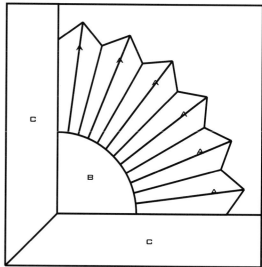

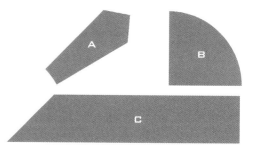

FANS IN BOXES

A delightfully easy way of adding a three-dimensional effect to quilts is to set the blocks into boxes, which can be adjusted to be as deep or as shallow as you wish. The sides of the box are drafted in exactly the same way as the frames in Attic Windows. Fan blocks look particularly good in this setting.

FABRICS

You will need six fabrics for this quilt—two light fabrics (Fabrics 1 and 4), a medium fabric (Fabric 2), a dark fabric (Fabric 3), a medium-dark fabric (Fabric 5), plus a background fabric (fabric 6) that can be either very dark or very light.

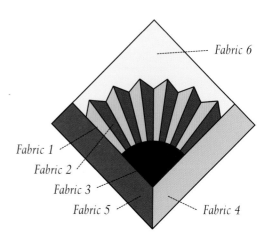

Fabric 6

Fabric 1
Fabric 2
Fabric 3
Fabric 5
Fabric 4

MAKING THE QUILT

STEP 1:

Following the instructions on page 21, make Templates A, B, and C, adding a ¼-inch (6-mm) seam allowance all around on each shape. Mark the center line on Template A.

STEP 2:

Cut out the fan blades using this quick-piece method: Cut 1-inch (2.5-cm) wide strips of Fabrics 1 and 2 (this includes seam allowance). Join the strips, taking a ¼-inch (6-mm) seam allowance, and press the seams open. Use Template A to cut six patches from each unit, aligning the center of the template with the seam line that joins the strips.

STEP 3:

Join the fan blades by placing them right sides together and stitching, using a ¼-inch (6-mm) seam.

STEP 4:

Using Template B, cut a patch from Fabric 3 and join it to the base of the fan. (See page 28 for instructions on sewing curves.) Alternatively, appliqué the base to the background square after the fans have been applied.

STEP 5:

Cut a piece of background fabric (Fabric 6) 10½ inches (26.5 cm) square. Appliqué the pieced fan to the square, turning under a ¼-inch (6-mm) seam allowance on each blade.

STEP 6:

Using Template C, cut one patch from Fabric 4. Reverse Template C and cut one patch from Fabric 5. Join these pieces to the sides of the box, mitering the corners where they meet (see Mitering on page 33).

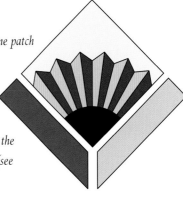

STEP 7:

Join the blocks in rows, following the instructions on page 31 for setting blocks "on point." Complete the rows by adding plain triangles. To make the triangles, cut 10½ inch (26.5 cm) squares in half diagonally. Finish by binding edges as shown on page 38.

Completed Fans in Boxes quilt top, using eighteen blocks.

Draft the pattern on a 12 x 12 square grid, as shown below.

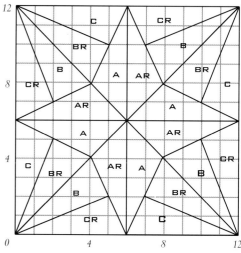

Only three templates are needed (A, B, and C), but each must be reversed to make up the pattern.

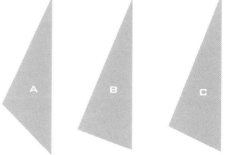

BLAZING STAR

The dimensional illusion in these star designs is achieved by dividing each ray into two halves, one light and one dark. The faceted rays make the star stand out from its background. A single block makes a striking wall hanging, while repeating the blocks gives added complexity to the design, as subpatterns are formed where the blocks meet. This is a superb pattern for a bed quilt.

FABRICS

You need three fabrics for this pattern—a dark fabric (Fabric 1) for the background, and medium and light fabrics (Fabrics 2 and 3) for the star. Fabrics 2 and 3 can be different tones of the same color if you wish.

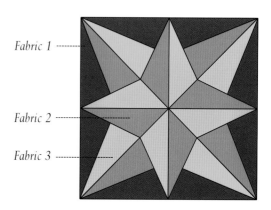

Fabric 1 --------

Fabric 2 --------

Fabric 3 --------

MAKING THE QUILT

STEP 1:

Following the instructions on page 21, make templates A, B, and C, adding a ¼-inch (6-mm) seam allowance all around on each shape.

STEP 2:

Using Template A, cut four patches from Fabric 2, then reverse the template and cut four patches from Fabric 3. Using Template B, cut four patches from Fabric 2, then reverse the template and cut four patches from Fabric 3. Using Template C, cut four patches from Fabric 1 and then reverse the template and cut another four patches from Fabric 1.

STEP 3:

Piece four identical units as shown.

STEP 4:

Join the four units to complete the block.

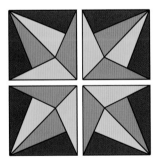 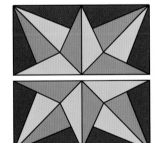

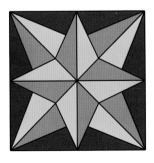

STEP 5:

Join repeated blocks to make the quilt. To finish, add mitered borders, as shown on page 33, or finish the edges by binding or butting as shown on page 38.

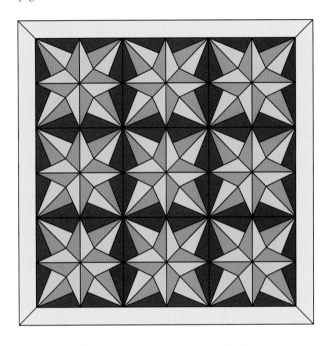

Completed Blazing Star quilt top with mitered borders.

BLAZING STAR WALL HANGING

To make a single Blazing Star block as a wall hanging, add mitered borders to the block, and finish by binding or butting (see page 38).

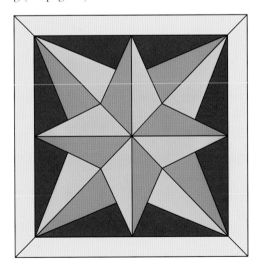

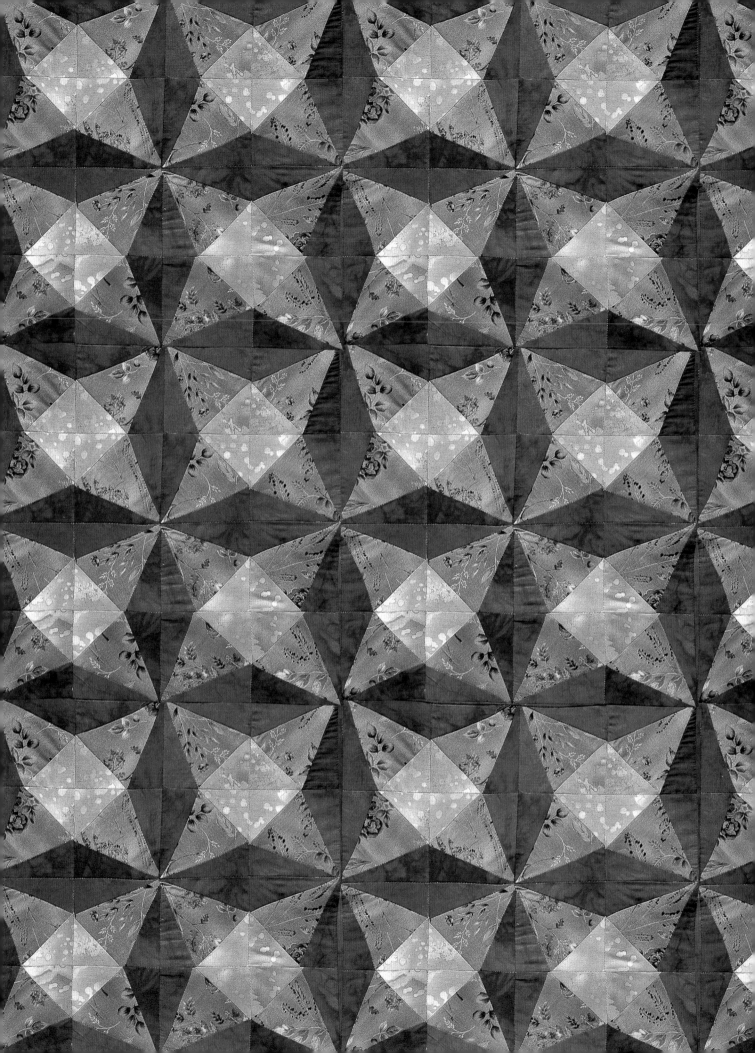

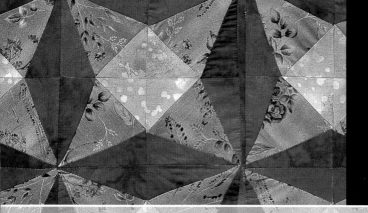

CIRCLES AND CURVES

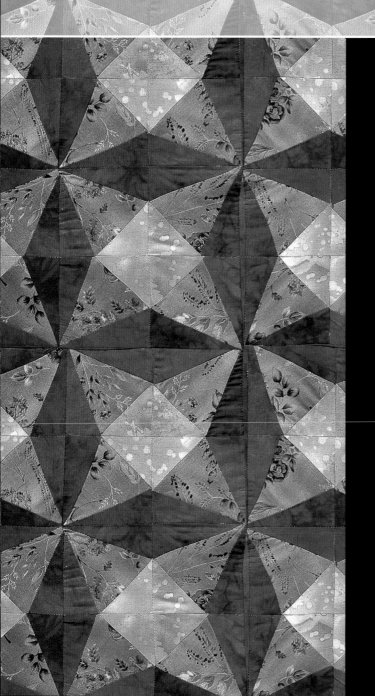

Many traditional American quilt blocks, when repeated, create the illusion of interlocking circles over the entire quilt surface. This effect looks all the more mysterious when the blocks are constructed without any curved seams. The secret lies in very simple geometry and results from the juxtaposition of certain angles, which deceives the eye into seeing them as being joined to create circles. Other patchwork techniques using only straight lines can also result in an impression of curves and swirls over the quilt surface, as seen in Twisted Log Cabin.

The basis of this pattern is eight triangles in alternating light and dark colors, pieced together to form an octagon. Four smaller triangles are then added to the corners to make a square.

The easiest way to draft all Kaleidosope blocks is on a 24 x 24 square grid, as shown below.

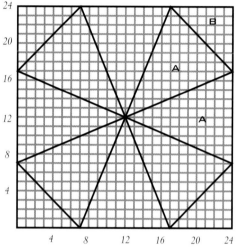

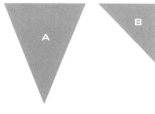

KALEIDOSCOPE

Even at its simplest, the Kaleidoscope block creates graphic effects of great complexity. By playing with the colors and their positioning, even more illusions can easily be created, making the Kaleidoscope one of the finest of all the eye-fooler blocks.

FOUR-POINTED STAR KALEIDOSCOPE

This quilt uses the basic Kaleidoscope block. The four-pointed star effect is greatly enhanced when half-blocks are added on all sides. The quilt "frame" is achieved by careful placement of patches around the edges of the blocks.

FABRICS

Scrap fabrics work well as long as they have a strong light/dark contrast. In the quilt shown, scrap fabrics have been used in shades of red, green, and blue, but you could use just two colors for the main blocks if you wish.

MAKING THE QUILT

STEP 1:

Following the drafting instructions on page 21, make templates A and B, adding a ¼-inch (6-mm) seam allowance all around on each shape.

STEP 2:

For each block, using Template A, cut four light and four dark triangles. Next, using Template B, cut four light triangles.

STEP 3:

Piece the block in two halves, alternating the light and dark A triangles. Join the halves to make an octagon.

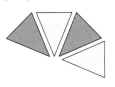 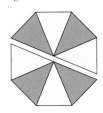

STEP 4:

Add the small B triangles to the four corners.

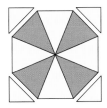 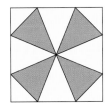

STEP 5:

Sew the blocks together in rows.

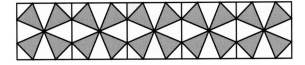

STEP 6:

To make the basic quilt top, join the rows together.

CHANGING FOCUS

The complexity of the Four-Pointed Star Kaleidoscope is increased by adding half-blocks to the edges of the basic design. To make a half-block, you will need to cut a Template A patch in half and piece as shown.

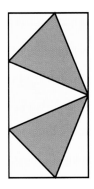

Add half-blocks to each end of the rows of blocks, and then to the top and bottom raw edges.

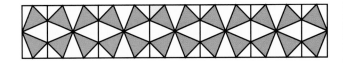

Completed Four-Pointed Star Kaleidoscope, edged with half-blocks

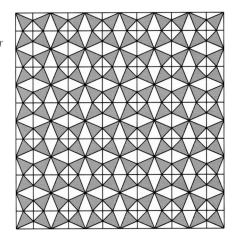

The Four-Pointed Star Kaleidoscope pattern can be further enhanced by using more colors.

CIRCLE-FOCUSED KALEIDOSCOPE

In this quilt, darker corners draw the eye toward the interlocking circular elements in the design.

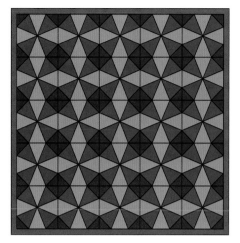

To make this quilt, proceed exactly as for the Four-Pointed Star quilt, but add a very dark fabric for the Template B triangles to the corners.

SQUARE-FOCUSED KALEIDOSCOPE

Adding light corners to the dark triangles emphasizes the squares.

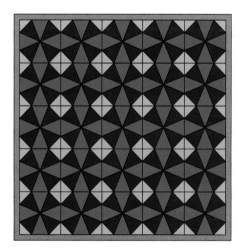

To make this quilt, proceed exactly as for the Four-Pointed Star quilt but add light-colored fabric corner B triangles to dark center A triangles.

SPIDER'S WEB KALEIDOSCOPE

This interesting version of the Kaleidoscope quilt can be made in two ways: You can make templates for the striped triangles in the usual way or you can use the strip-piecing method shown here to piece lots of triangles quickly and easily.

STRIP-PIECING METHOD

The quilt is easiest to work in 12-inch (30-cm) blocks. Each of the pieced strips will make eight triangles. These, when combined with eight solid dark triangles, will make two blocks (Block A and Block B). You can then combine the two blocks to make a quilt. Work out the overall size you want for the finished quilt and then calculate the number of blocks you need. From this you can calculate exactly how many pieced strips you need to make.

Block A

Block B

FABRICS

You will need three fabrics for this quilt—one medium and one light fabric (Fabrics 1 and 2) for the striped triangles, and one dark fabric (Fabric 3) for the solid triangles.

MAKING THE QUILT

STEP 1:

Draft the block as for the basic Kaleidoscope block (see page 63).

STEP 2:

Make Templates A and B as for the basic Kaleidoscope block (see page 63).

STEP 3:

Cut two strips 1½ inches (3.75 cm) wide and 16 inches (40 cm) long from Fabrics 1 and 2.

STEP 4:

Join the strips, alternating the colors. Press the seams to one side.

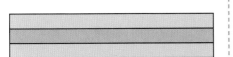

STEP 5:

Using Template A, cut triangles from the strip-pieced fabric, turning the template for each cut, so that the fabric is not wasted.

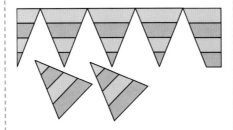

STEP 6:

Using Template A, cut eight patches from Fabric 3.

STEP 7:

Using Template B, cut eight corner triangles from Fabric 3.

STEP 8:

Join the triangles, alternating pieced triangles that have a light strip at their base with solid ones, to make Block A. Add corners to the solid triangles.

STEP 9:

Join the remaining four pieced and four solid triangles and add corner triangles to complete Block B.

STEP 10:

Sew the blocks together, alternating Blocks A and B to make the quilt top.

SPIDER'S WEB VARIATION

For an even more complex-looking quilt, make all the large triangular sections with striped fabric.

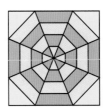

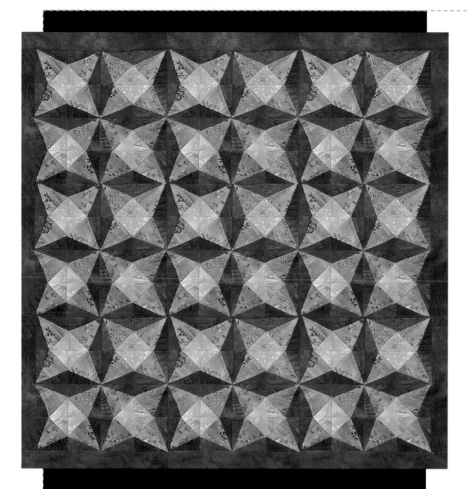

DIAMOND STAR

Diamond Star developed from a block known as World Without End, a four-pointed star drafted on an 8 x 8 square grid. When four blocks are joined they form Diamond Star, which, when repeated, reveals both stars and circles.

Although the block looks very complex, it is, in fact, pieced from these four identical units and needs only three templates and three fabrics.

Draft the block on a 8 x 8 square grid, as shown below.

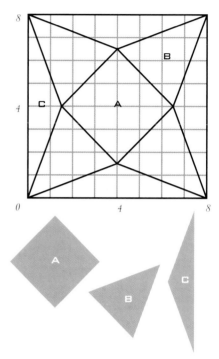

Note that the four triangles on the sides of each unit are set in. Full instructions for doing this are given on page 27, but remember that the important thing is to sew up to, but not into, the seam allowances. Sew the first seam, then pivot the patch to sew the second one.

FABRICS

You need three fabrics for this pattern—light fabric (Fabric 1) for the square, a medium-light fabric (Fabric 2) for the inner triangles, and a dark fabric (Fabric 3) for the outer triangles.

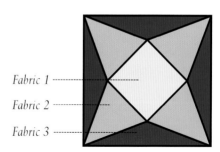

Fabric 1 ....
Fabric 2 ....
Fabric 3 ....

MAKING THE QUILT

STEP 1:

Following the instructions on page 21, make Templates A, B, and C, adding a ¼-inch (6-mm) seam allowance all around on all shapes.

STEP 2:

Using Template A, cut one patch from Fabric 1.

STEP 3:

Using Template B, cut four patches from Fabric 2.

STEP 4:

Using Template C, cut four patches from Fabric 3.

STEP 5:

Join one Template B patch to each side of the Template A square, taking care not to stitch into the seam allowance at the bottom of each triangle.

STEP 6:

Set in a Fabric 3 patch in the center of each side. Stitch up to the seam allowance on one side of each patch, then pivot the patch and sew up the other side. Make three more units in this way.

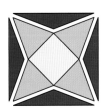

STEP 7:

Join the units to make the block.

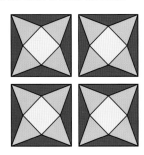 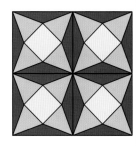

STEP 8:

Join repeated blocks to make the quilt. To finish, add plain borders as shown on page 32.

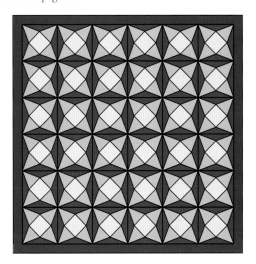

Completed Diamond Star quilt top with plain borders.

DIAMOND STAR VARIATION

You can create a very different effect for the Diamond Star quilt by simply reversing the placement of the dark and light fabrics.

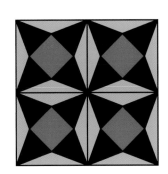

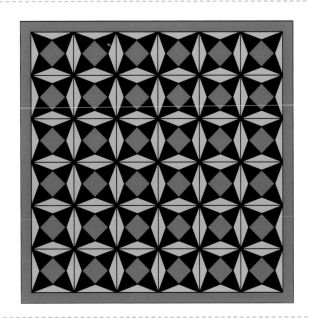

Storm at Sea is a four-patch block drafted on a 16 x 16 square grid. Although seven templates are needed, it is very straightforward to piece.

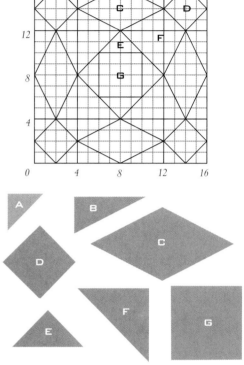

STORM AT SEA

The appropriately named Storm at Sea produces intriguingly complex patterns over the quilt surface. The way you manipulate the colors offers many design possibilities. Looked at in one way, a pattern of undulating waves emerges—hence the name. From another perspective, interlocking circles can be seen. These effects are caused by the positioning of the long diamonds on four sides of the block and also by the color placement.

FABRICS

At its simplest the block needs only four fabrics, as in the quilt shown, yet the graphic impact is still strong. Choose two medium shades (Fabric 1, Fabric 4), a dark one (Fabric 2), and a light one (Fabric 3). Traditionally, Storm at Sea quilts tend to be pieced in blue fabrics, echoing the associations conjured up by the name.

Fabric 1
Fabric 2
Fabric 3
Fabric 4

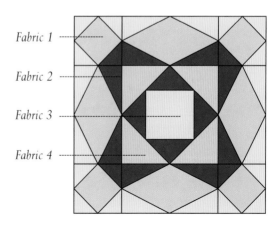

MAKING THE QUILT

STEP 1:

Following the instructions on page 21, make templates A–G, adding a ¼-inch (6-mm) seam allowance all around on all shapes.

STEP 2:

Using Template A, cut twelve patches from Fabric 3 and four from Fabric 2. Using Template B, cut eight patches from Fabric 2 and eight patches from Fabric 3. Using Template C, cut four patches from Fabric 1. Using Template D, cut four patches from Fabric 1. Using Template E, cut four patches from Fabric 2. Using Template F, cut four patches from Fabric 4. Using Template G, cut one patch from Fabric 3.

STEP 3:

Piece the units as shown below.

x 4

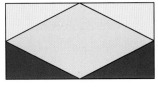

x 4

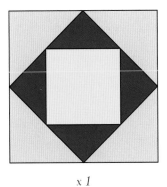

x 1

STEP 4:

Join the units as shown.

STEP 5:

To make the quilt, join the blocks in rows. Add mitered borders as shown on page 33.

Completed Storm at Sea quilt top. Increasing the number of blocks can have a dramatic effect.

Five templates (A, B, C, D, and E) are needed for this design. Draft the block on an 18 x 18 square grid, as shown below.

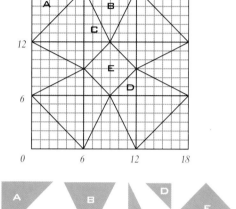

FABRICS

You need three fabrics for this pattern—a dark one (Fabric 1), a medium one (Fabric 2), and a light one (Fabric 3).

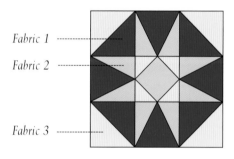

ROAD TO PARADISE

Road to Paradise is a simple nine-patch block that has great design potential. When blocks are repeated, a secondary pattern of diamonds emerges, which, in turn, creates the illusion of circles.

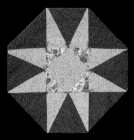

MAKING THE QUILT

STEP 1:

Following the instructions on page 21, make Templates A to E, adding a ¼-inch (6-mm) seam allowance all around on all shapes.

STEP 2:

Using Template A, cut four triangles from Fabric 1 and four from Fabric 3. Using Template B, cut four triangles from Fabric 1. Using Template C, cut eight triangles from Fabric 2. Using Template D, cut four triangles from Fabric 3. Using Template E cut one square from Fabric 2.

STEP 3:

Piece the following units.

x 4

x 4

x 1

STEP 4:

Join the units as shown below to make the block.

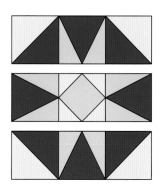

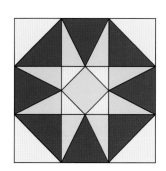

STEP 5:

Join the blocks to make the quilt. To finish, add plain borders as shown on page 32.

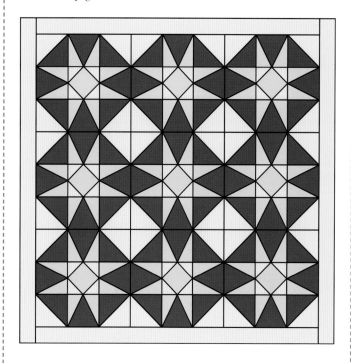

Completed Road to Pardise quilt top, using nine blocks.

ROAD TO PARADISE VARIATION

By changing the background color from light to dark, you can create a more dramatic effect.

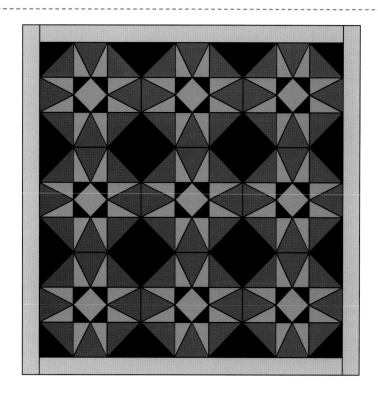

Adding a border in a contrasting color further enhances this variation.

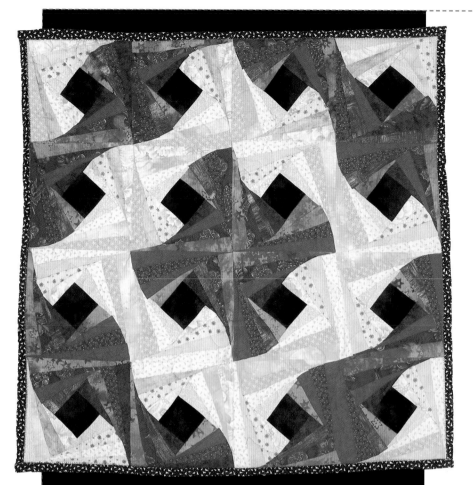

TWISTED LOG CABIN

*Also known as Revolving Log Cabin, this fascinating variation on the
traditional Log Cabin block can be used to produce convincing curved
effects—even though the block is pieced entirely with straight lines.
Once you've learned the method, you can add as many logs to your
block as you like.*

Several patterns can be made with Log Cabin
blocks, depending on how they are arranged.
In the quilt on the left, the blocks are
arranged in a pattern known as Barn Raising.
The Log Cabin block is made by sewing strips
of dark and light fabrics onto adjacent sides of
a square, as in the Traditional Log Cabin block
shown below. In Twisted Log Cabin the strips
are set at an angle.

Any number of strips can be added, but the
more strips there are, the more exaggerated
the curve will be. In this quilt, four strips
have been added to each side.

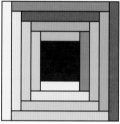
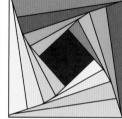

*Traditional Log
Cabin Block*

*Twisted Log
Cabin Block*

The easiest way to make these blocks is by
the foundation method (see page 29), in which
the pattern is marked on the foundation fabric
and the logs are sewn on the guidelines. No
templates are needed.

FABRICS

The two sides of each block must show a clear
contrast between dark and light fabrics,
although fabrics can be of mixed scraps
provided the contrast is clear.

MAKING THE QUILT

STEP 1:

Copy the foundation pattern as many times as you need. (You will need one pattern for each block.) To make an 8-inch (20-cm) block, enlarge the foundation block shown here by 400 percent.

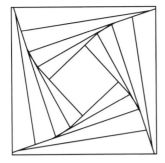

STEP 2:

If you are using scrap fabrics, sort your fabrics into dark and light groups.

STEP 3:

Make up the block, following the instructions for foundation piecing on page 29.

STEP 4:

When all the blocks are completed, lay them out on a flat surface and try them in different arrangements until you are satisfied with the result.

STEP 5:

Join the blocks to make a quilt top. After quilting, finish by binding or butting, as shown on page 38.

Completed Twisted Log Cabin quilt top in Barn Raising pattern.

TWISTED LOG CABIN VARIATION

In this quilt, the Twisted Log Cabin blocks have been arranged in a pattern known as Light and Dark, or Checkerboard.

This Twisted Log Cabin variation sets thirty-six blocks in the Light and Dark pattern.

COURTHOUSE STEPS BLOCK

In this block, the dark and light fabrics are placed on opposite sides of the square—unlike Log Cabin, where they are placed on adjacent sides.

In the quilt shown here, the Twisted Courthouse Steps blocks have been arranged in straight rows, resulting in a twisted ribbon effect.

Traditional Courthouse Steps Block

Twisted Courthouse Steps Block

Completed Twisted Courthouse Steps quilt top

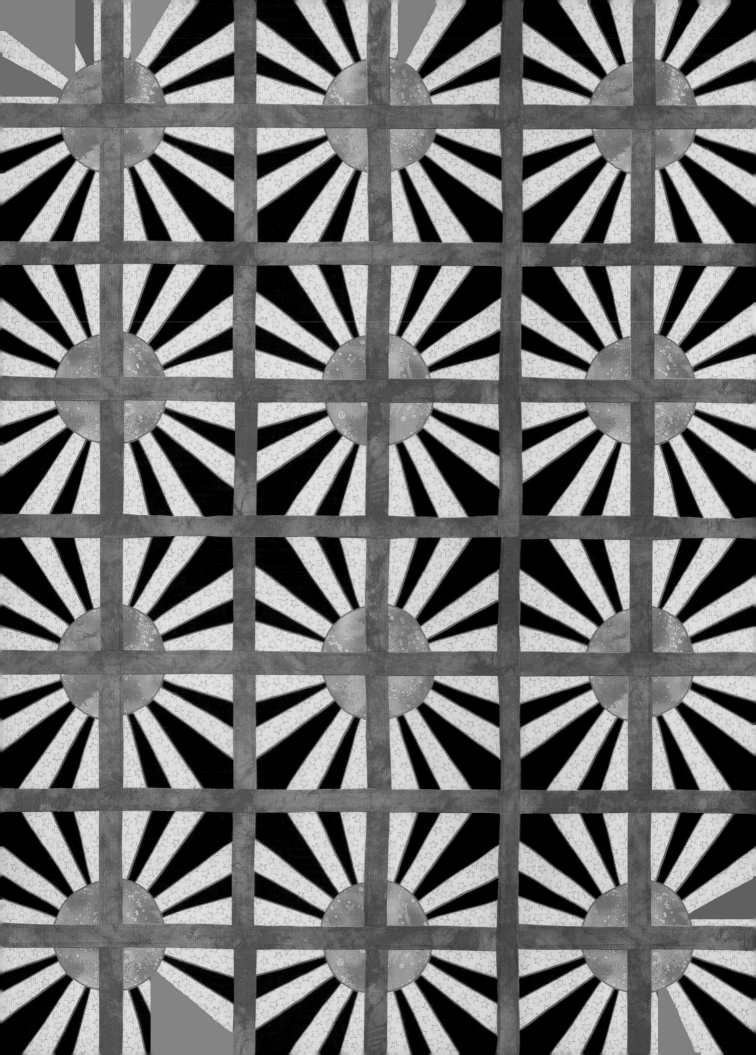

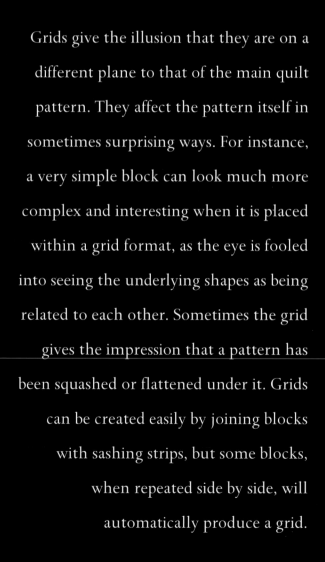

SECTION 3

GRIDS

Grids give the illusion that they are on a different plane to that of the main quilt pattern. They affect the pattern itself in sometimes surprising ways. For instance, a very simple block can look much more complex and interesting when it is placed within a grid format, as the eye is fooled into seeing the underlying shapes as being related to each other. Sometimes the grid gives the impression that a pattern has been squashed or flattened under it. Grids can be created easily by joining blocks with sashing strips, but some blocks, when repeated side by side, will automatically produce a grid.

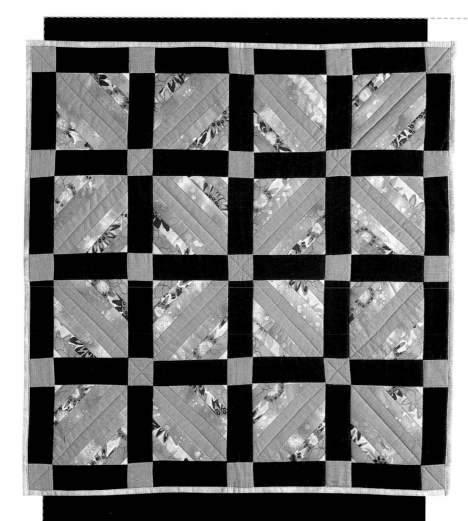

The quickest and easiest way to piece this block is to use the foundation method (see page 29), which does not require templates. Note that the center patch is wider than the others and provides a dominant feature of the pattern. It's essential, therefore, that you think carefully about the color for that patch and choose one that will stand out well under the grid.

FABRICS

Any number of colors that go well together can be used for the strips.

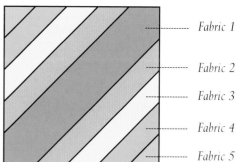

Fabric 1
Fabric 2
Fabric 3
Fabric 4
Fabric 5

MAKING THE QUILT

STEP 1:

Enlarge the foundation block above by 400 percent. This will produce a block with a 6-inch (15-cm) finished size. Prepare foundations for the number of blocks you need. You can either photocopy the pattern as many times as necessary or trace the pattern onto each square.

STEP 2:

Select a fabric (Fabric 1) for the center patch, and four others (Fabrics 2, 3, 4, and 5) that will complement it.

LATTICED SQUARES

This very simply constructed block can produce several illusions. The blocks are all pieced identically, but alternate blocks are rotated to create the effect of strip-pieced squares, which are then overlaid by a strong grid.

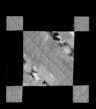

76

STEP 3:

Cut out fabric for the center patch, making sure that it is wide enough to cover the marked lines.

STEP 4:

Cut strips of Fabrics 2, 3, 4, and 5, making them 1 inch (2.5 cm) wider than the strips marked on the foundation square. Lay them on the foundation square to see roughly how long they should be, but cut them to a generous length because you will cut off any excess later. The strips will get shorter toward the edges of the square.

STEP 5:

Place the Fabric 1 strip diagonally on the foundation square from corner to corner and pin it in place.

STEP 6:

Following the foundation piecing method, take a Fabric 2 strip and lay it on top of the Fabric 1 strip, putting right sides and raw edges together. Pin it into position. Turn to the back and stitch along the marked line. Turn to front and press the strip open.

STEP 7:

Repeat Step 6 with a second Fabric 2 strip, sewing it to the other side of the center strip.

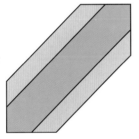

STEP 8:

Continue in this way, adding Fabric 3, 4, and 5 strips on either side of the block. As you pin each strip into position, turn to the back and check that the marked stitching line is covered. You can do this by holding the foundation up to the light.

STEP 9:

When all strips have been added, press the block from the front. Turn to the back of the block and trim the strips even with the foundation. If you have used paper foundations, tear them away from the seams and remove them now.

STEP 10:

Lay out the blocks, rotating them so that the strips form squares.

STEP 11:

Join the blocks with sashings and posts, following the instructions on page 31. You can emphasize the effect of the underlying squares even more by using narrower sashings, which will bring the blocks closer to each other.

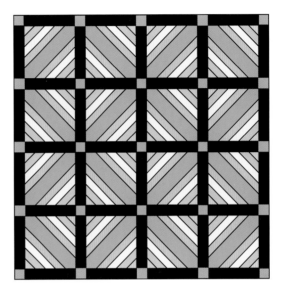

Completed Latticed Squares quilt top.

STREAK O' LIGHTNING VARIATION

In this example, the blocks have been rotated to reveal a Streak o' Lightning pattern—a zig-zag effect—underneath the grid.

Latticed Squares variation with plain sashings.

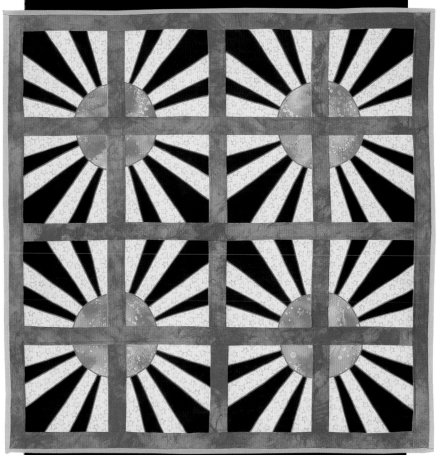

Draft the block on a 16 x 16 square grid, as shown below, using a compass to draw the arc at the base.

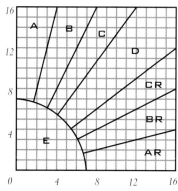

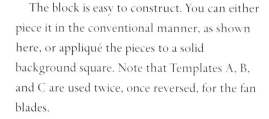

The block is easy to construct. You can either piece it in the conventional manner, as shown here, or appliqué the pieces to a solid background square. Note that Templates A, B, and C are used twice, once reversed, for the fan blades.

FABRICS

You will need four fabrics for the block—one light-medium (Fabric 1), one dark (Fabric 2), and one medium-dark (Fabric 3), plus a contrasting fabric for the sashing that forms the grid.

HARVEST SUN

When this easy fan block is joined with sashing, two illusions appear: Sun rays splash out from beneath the grid, and four-pointed stars appear at alternate junctions.

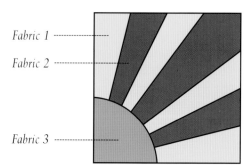

Fabric 1 --------
Fabric 2 --------
Fabric 3 --------

TO MAKE THE QUILT

STEP 1:

Following the instructions on page 21, make Templates A–E, adding a ¼-inch (6-mm) seam allowance all around on each shape.

STEP 2:

Using Template A, cut one patch of Fabric 1. Then reverse the Template and cut another Fabric 1 patch.

STEP 3:

Using Template B, cut one patch from Fabric 2. Then reverse the template and cut another Fabric 2 patch.

STEP 4:

Using Template C, cut one patch from Fabric 1. Then reverse the template and cut another Fabric 1 patch.

STEP 5:

Using Template D, cut one patch from Fabric 2.

STEP 6:

Using Template E, cut one patch from Fabric 3.

STEP 7:

Piece the fan blades and then add the arc (Template E) at the base (See Sewing curves on page 28).

STEP 8:

Lay out the blocks, rotating them to form the "sun." Join the blocks with narrow sashings, following the instructions on page 30. Complete the top by adding sashing strips to all four sides.

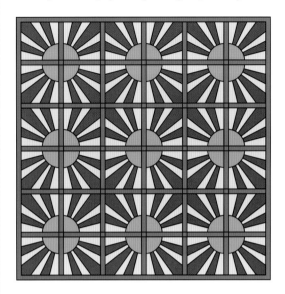

Completed Harvest Sun quilt top, using thirty-six blocks.

CHANGING EMPHASIS

In the quilt shown above, the black rays dominate the relatively medium tone of the grid, emphasizing the pattern of the pieced blocks. Changing the tones so that the grid is dark places the emphasis on the grid.

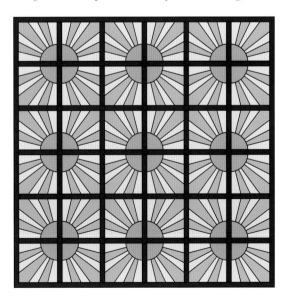

Harvest Sun quilt top under a dark grid.

KING DAVID'S CROWN

Another very simple traditional four-patch block, King David's Crown produces large, four-pointed stars lying under a grid when the blocks are repeated. The kaleidoscope blocks present a bewildering choice of stars and circles for the eye to focus on. Using two shades of color for the cross creates the effect of different strips placed one over the other to create the grid.

Draft this block on a 24 x 24 square grid, as shown below.

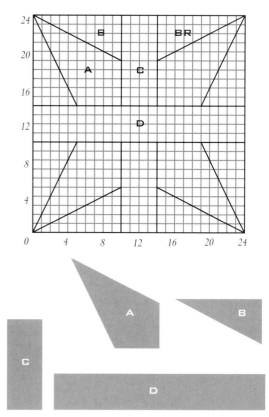

FABRICS

You will need four fabrics for this design—a dark fabric for the background of the star (Fabric 1), a medium fabric for the star itself (Fabric 2), and a medium-dark (Fabric 3) and a light fabric (Fabric 4) for the cross.

Fabric 1
Fabric 2
Fabric 3
Fabric 4

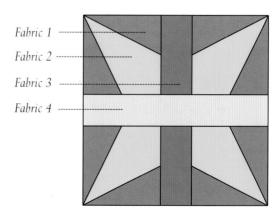

MAKING THE QUILT

STEP 1:

Following the instructions on page 21, make Templates A–D, adding a ¼-inch (6-mm) seam allowance around each shape.

STEP 2:

Using Template A, cut four patches in Fabric 2. Cut four patches in Fabric 1 using Template B and BR. Using Template C, cut two patches in Fabric 3. Using Template D, cut one patch in Fabric 4.

STEP 3:

Using the A and B patches, piece four units as shown.

 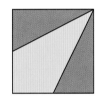

x 4

STEP 4:

Join the units in pairs with the Template C patches.

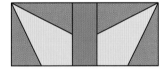 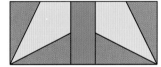

STEP 5:

Join the paired units with the template D patch.

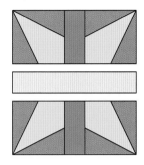 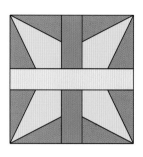

STEP 6:

Join the blocks in rows and add plain borders to finish, as shown on page 32.

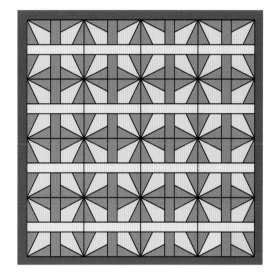

Completed King David's Crown quilt top, using sixteen blocks.

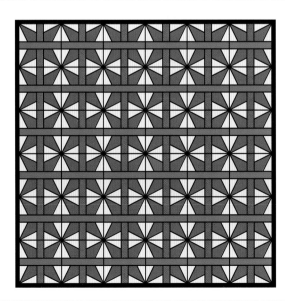

KING DAVID'S CROWN VARIATION

This quilt looks completely different when a light background is used for the four triangles in the block.

King David's Crown increases in complexity when more blocks are added. This illustration shows thirty-six blocks.

Draft the block on a 10 x 10 square grid, as shown below. Three templates are needed.

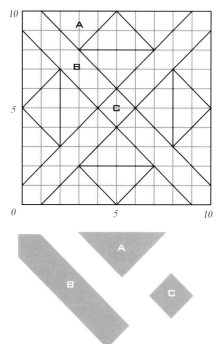

FABRICS

Four fabrics are needed—a medium one (Fabric 1), a dark one (Fabric 2), and two light ones (Fabrics 3 and 4).

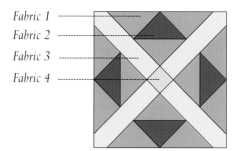

Fabric 1
Fabric 2
Fabric 3
Fabric 4

MAKING THE QUILT

STEP 1:

Following the instructions on page 21, make Templates A, B, and C, adding a ¼-inch (6-mm) seam allowance all around on each shape.

STEP 2:

Using Template A, cut twelve patches in Fabric 1 and four patches in Fabric 2. Using Template B, cut four patches in Fabric 3. Using Template C, cut one patch in Fabric 4.

ALL KINDS

Many five- and seven-patch blocks have a center bar, which can be solid or pieced. Some of the solid-bar blocks give the illusion of a pieced block lying beneath a grid. This block, a variation on the traditional one known as All Kinds, is a good example. Repeated blocks reveal an Ohio Star lying beneath the grid.

STEP 3:

Piece four triangular
units, as shown.

x 4

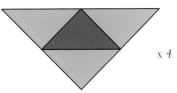

STEP 4:

Join two triangular units with a Template B patch.
Repeat with the other two triangular units.

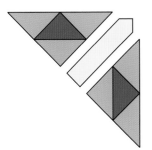 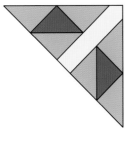

STEP 5:

Join the remaining Template B patches to the Template C patch to
make the center strip, then join the two halves of the block.

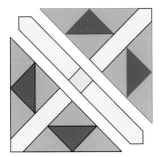 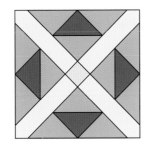

STEP 6:

Finish with plain borders (see page 32) or, after quilting, finish the
edges by binding or butting (see page 38).

Completed All Kinds quilt top with plain borders.

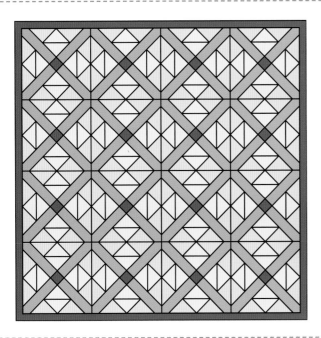

ALL KINDS VARIATION

A very small change to the coloring of the patches in
All Kinds leads to a completely different quilt, in
which the underlying pattern of squares is dominant.

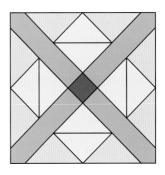

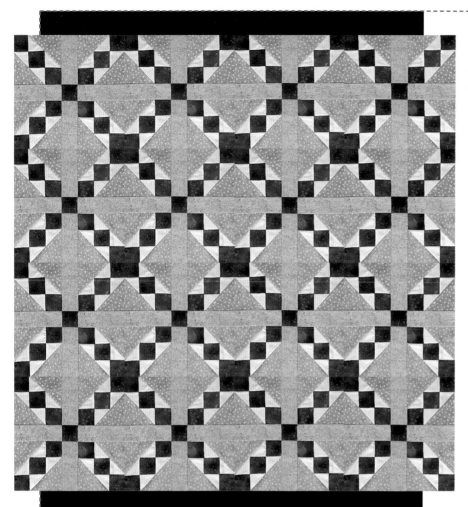

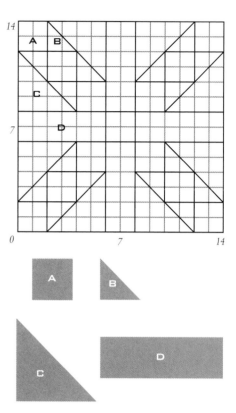

Draft the block on a 14 x 14 square grid, as shown below.

COUNTRY ROADS

A repeated seven-patch block reveals an underlying pattern of a diagonal pieced grid.

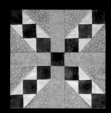

FABRICS

You need four fabrics for this design—a dark one (Fabric 1), a light one (Fabric 2), a medium-dark one (Fabric 3), and a medium-light one (Fabric 4).

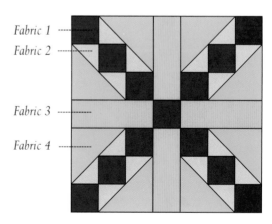

Fabric 1
Fabric 2
Fabric 3
Fabric 4

MAKING THE QUILT

STEP 1:

Following the instructions on page 21, make Templates A–D, adding a ¼-inch (6-mm) seam allowance around each shape.

STEP 2:

Using Template A, cut thirteen patches from Fabric 1. Using Template B, cut sixteen patches from Fabric 2. Using Template C, cut eight patches from Fabric 4. Using Template D, cut four patches from Fabric 3.

STEP 3:

Piece four units as shown below.

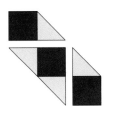 

x 4

STEP 4:

To make the block, join the units with the four D pieces and the remaining A piece, as shown below.

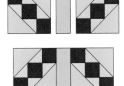 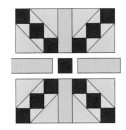

STEP 5:

Join the blocks in rows to make the quilt top. After quilting, finish the edges by binding or butting.

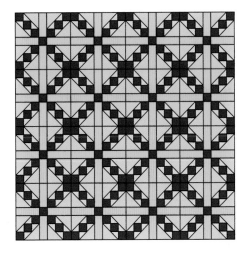

Completed Country Roads quilt top.

COUNTRY ROADS VARIATION

The quilt achieves greater complexity when the blocks are set "on point." Each row is completed with half-blocks and with quarter-blocks at the corners, forming an attractive sawtooth border. The half-blocks must be pieced in a different way from the quilt above to achieve this effect.

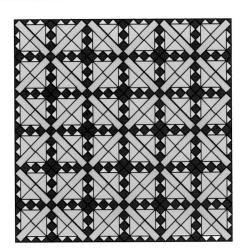

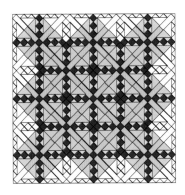

Piece the half-blocks as shown.

Piece the quarter-blocks as shown.

Although the piecing of the block looks dauntingly complicated at first glance, it is really quite straightforward. Draft it on a 24 x 24 square grid, as shown below.

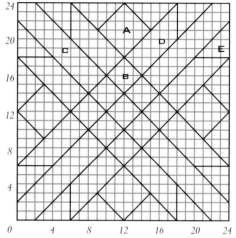

RAILROAD CROSSING

In one interpretation of this complex-looking block, eight-pointed stars can be seen. Look again and you can see patterns of squares.

FABRICS

You need four fabrics for this design—one dark (Fabric 1), one light (Fabric 2), one medium-dark (Fabric 3), and one medium-light (Fabric 4).

Fabric 1 --------
Fabric 2 --------

Fabric 3 --------

Fabric 4 --------

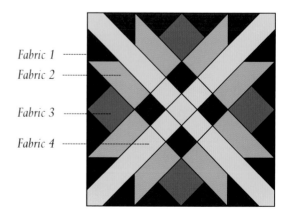

MAKING THE QUILT

STEP 1:

Following the instructions on page 21, make Templates A–E, adding a ¼-inch (6-mm) seam allowance all around on all shapes.

STEP 2:

Using Template A, cut four patches from Fabric 3. Using Template B, cut four patches from Fabric 1 and five from Fabric 4. Using Template C, cut four patches from Fabric 4. Using Template D, cut four patches from Fabric 2 and then reverse the Template and cut another four patches from Fabric 2. Using Template E, cut sixteen patches from Fabric 1.

STEP 3:

Piece the following units.

x 4

x 4

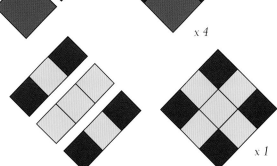

x 1

STEP 4:

Join the units as shown.

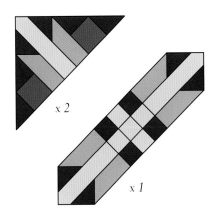

x 2

x 1

STEP 5:

Assemble the block as shown below.

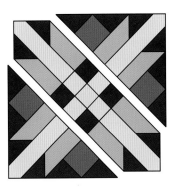

STEP 6:

Repeat the blocks to make the quilt, and add plain borders as shown on page 32.

Completed Railroad Crossing quilt top, using sixteen blocks.

Ombre is an easy five-patch block that can be pieced from half-square triangles and squares. The template-free method, described on page 41, is ideal for this block, but, if you prefer to use templates, you will need three—A, B and C. Draft the block on a 5 x 5 square grid, as shown below.

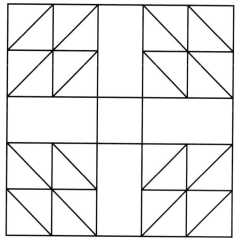

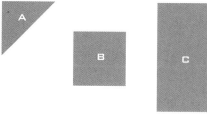

FABRICS

You will need five fabrics for this design. Any fabrics who's tones work well together can be chosen, or you can shade fabrics from light to dark from one corner of the square to the other.

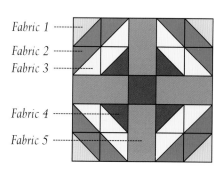

Fabric 1
Fabric 2
Fabric 3

Fabric 4
Fabric 5

OMBRE

Ombre is a variation of the block known as Handy Andy. It appears in only one reference book, and whether the name is meant to suggest the shaded coloring of the block or the old card game Ombre is a mystery!

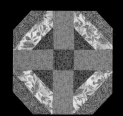

MAKING THE QUILT

STEP 1:

Following the instructions on page 21, make templates A, B, and C, adding a ¼-inch (6-mm) seam allowance all around each shape.

STEP 2:

Using Template A, cut four patches from Fabric 1, twelve from Fabric 2, twelve from Fabric 3 and four from Fabric 4. Using Template B, cut one patch from Fabric 4. Using Template C, cut four patches from Fabric 5. Join the patches to make the units below.

x 4   x 4   x 8   x 1   x 4

STEP 3:

Join the Template A patches to make four four-square units as shown below.

 x 4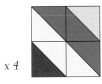

STEP 4:

Join two of the four-square units with a Template C patch. Repeat with the other two units.

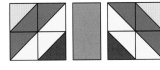

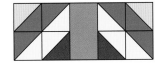

STEP 5:

Join two Template C patches to the Template B patch to make the center strip, then join the two halves to complete the block.

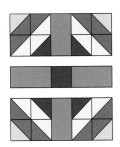 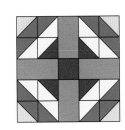

STEP 5:

Join blocks in rows. After quilting, finish the edges by binding.

Completed Ombre quilt top, using sixteen blocks.

OMBRE VARIATION

Using shaded tones of a single color creates a more subtle effect. Remember, though, that monochrome quilts like this need very carefully chosen colors, with sufficient contrast between the shades to bring out the pattern.

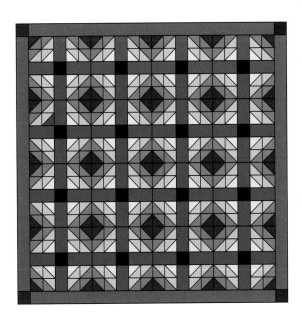

Ombre monochrome variation with border and corner posts.

INTERLACING

Interlaced lines and shapes are a decorative feature in many cultures and traditions. From Celtic knot patterns to the geometrically complex Moorish designs seen on tiles and screens, they tantalize the eye as they weave in and out, over and under. These effects are seen to wonderful effect in several traditional patchwork patterns and blocks and are also a constant source of inspiration to contemporary quilt makers, some of whom have worked out ingenious but accessible ways of piecing the patterns.

The method for piecing this particular interlaced star comes from the American quilt artist Margit Echols, who spent a great deal of time researching and adapting this and other patterns to use in her quilts. The interlacing effect is created through the use of a dark and a light tone of the same color.

The principle is very simple. Rows of identical pieced triangles are joined together, with alternate units turned upside down to form the pattern.

Draft the pattern on an isometric grid, as shown below. You can make the triangles any size you wish by scaling up or down on the grid. The quilt illustrated contains twenty-four triangles, but you can adjust the number to make a quilt of any size you like.

Template plastic, made especially for quilters, comes marked with an isometric grid. It is ideal for this pattern because it allows you to draw straight onto the plastic and cut out along the lines to make accurate templates.

ORIENTAL STAR

Some of the finest and most intricate examples of interlacing are
found in Moorish art, epitomized by the floor and wall tiles and
wooden screens that decorate the famous Moorish palace, the
Alhambra, in Granada, Spain. The sheer mathematical complexity of
some of these designs is awe-inspiring, yet with a little understanding
of the underlying principles, and some ingenuity, many of them can be
adapted for pieced patchwork.

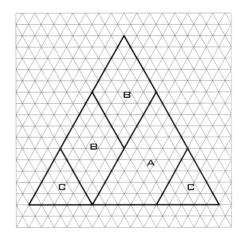

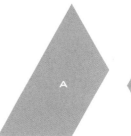

FABRICS

You will need four fabrics for this pattern—a light fabric (Fabric 1), a darker tone of the same color (Fabric 2), a medium-dark fabric (Fabric 3), and a medium-light fabric (Fabric 4). Fabrics 1 and 2 create the interlacing effect.

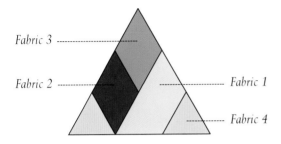

MAKING THE QUILT

STEP 1:

Following the instructions on page 21, draft the pattern and make Templates A, B, and C, adding a ¼-inch (6-mm) seam allowance all around on each one.

STEP 2:

Using Template A, cut one patch from Fabric 1. Using Template B, cut one patch from Fabric 2 and one from Fabric 3. Using Template C, cut two patches from Fabric 4.

STEP 3:

Make twenty-four triangle blocks, as shown below.

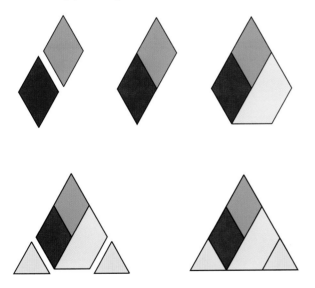

STEP 4:

Join the triangles in four rows, rotating them to form the pattern. There are five triangles in the first row, seven in the second row, seven in the third row, and five in the fourth row.

STEP 5:

Complete the quilt top by adding mitered borders, as shown on page 33.

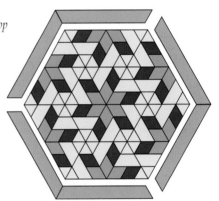

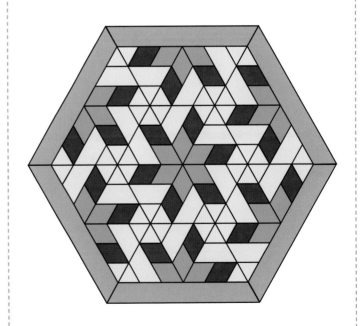

Completed Oriental Star quilt top, using twenty-four triangles.

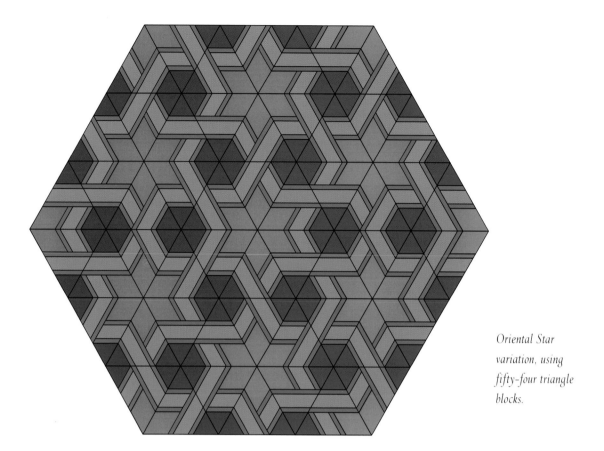

*Oriental Star
variation, using
fifty-four triangle
blocks.*

ORIENTAL STAR VARIATION

To create the interlacing effect in the variation, you need
only three fabrics, one of which should have a clear stripe
or directional pattern; border fabrics are a good choice.

FABRICS

You will need three fabrics for this variation—a striped
fabric (Fabric 1), a medium-light fabric (Fabric 2), and a
medium-dark fabric (Fabric 3).

When cutting patches from Fabric 1 (the striped fabric),
take note of the direction in which the stripes run along
the templates. The templates must be used in the same
direction each time, with the stripe running exactly the
same way in each patch. The size of the quilt is a personal
choice; this quilt has fifty-four triangles in it.

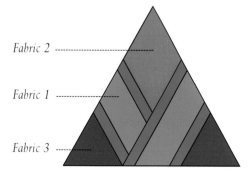

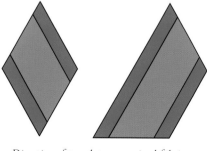

Direction of templates on striped fabric

MAKING THE QUILT

STEP 1:

Make templates A, B, and C as on page 92. Using template A, cut one patch from Fabric 1. Using Template B, cut one patch from Fabric 1 and one from Fabric 2. Using Template C, cut two patches from Fabric 3.

STEP 2.

Proceed exactly as for the first version of Oriental Star (see pages 92–93), piecing the triangles as shown.

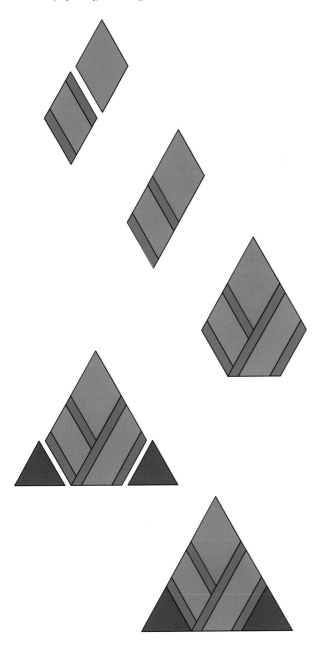

STEP 3:

Make fifty-four triangle blocks and lay them out in six rows, rotating alternate triangles to form the stars. There are seven triangles in the first row, nine in the second, eleven in the third, eleven in the fourth, nine in the fifth, and seven in the sixth.

STEP 4:

Join the triangles into rows and then join the rows as shown below.

STEP 5:

Complete the quilt top by binding or butting the edges (see page 38).

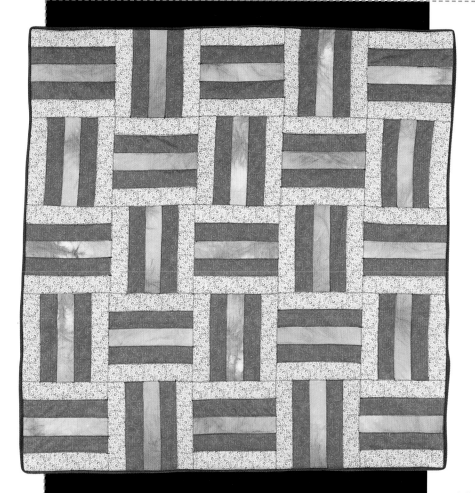

This Rail Fence quilt does not require templates. Any number of strips can be used, the only rule being that the block must be square.

For example, five 2-inch (5-cm) strips (finished size) will produce a band that is 10 inches (25 cm) wide, so the band must be cut to make 10-inch (25-cm) squares. If the band is made up of an odd number of strips, the interwoven effect is enhanced by using a strong color for the center strip with two other colors placed symmetrically on either side, as in the five-strip version shown here.

FABRICS

You can use any number of fabrics and colors for this pattern. The version here uses only three.

RAIL FENCE

One of the easiest yet most effective ways to make a quick quilt, Rail Fence is a favorite traditional one-patch block for creating woven effects. Simply join strips of fabric of the same width to make a band, and cut the band into squares.

MAKING THE QUILT

STEP 1:
Cut five strips of fabric to the required width.

STEP 2:
Join the strips using accurate ¼-inch (6-mm) seams. Press the seams open.

STEP 3:
Measure the width of the band. Measure along the band and cut pieces to the same measurement as the width, to make squares.

STEP 4:

Lay out the squares in rows, alternating the direction of each one to form the woven effect.

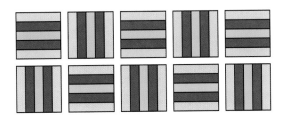

STEP 5:

Join the blocks in rows, then join the rows. To complete the quilt top, add a border with corner posts or finish by binding.

Completed Rail Fence quilt top, using twenty-five squares of five strips.

RAIL FENCE VARIATIONS

More complex effects can be created by increasing the number of strips. Seven are used in the quilt shown to the right.

In the two quilts shown below, each square contains six strips, but in the one on the right a strong color has been used in the last strip in the block. This produces "steps" across the quilt surface—a very popular and effective use of the Rail Fence block. Note, however, that it detracts from the woven effect.

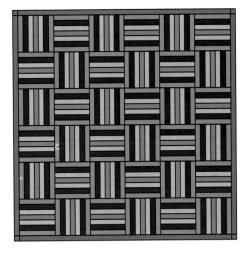

The block is constructed from two basic units plus the center square, and the whole secret of the interlaced effect lies in the color placement. This is where you need to be able to judge the relative tones of fabrics, using one of the methods described on page 13. The important point is that Fabrics 1 and 2 must be of significantly contrasting dark and light tones. Provided you get that contrast, the woven effect will appear when the blocks are joined in rows.

Five templates (A, B, C, D, and E) are required for this design. Draft the block on an 18 x 18 square grid, as shown below.

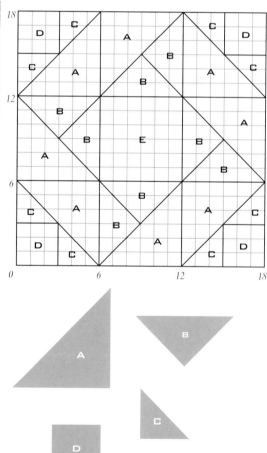

NINE-PATCH WEAVE

Nine-Patch Weave demonstrates the design strengths of the simple nine-patch block, the versatility of which seems infinite. In this version, it's difficult to see at first glance that the complex interwoven effect is produced simply by repeating identical blocks.

FABRICS

You need five fabrics for this pattern—a dark fabric (Fabric 1), a medium-light fabric (Fabric 2), a light fabric (Fabric 3), a medium-dark fabric (Fabric 4), and a medium fabric (Fabric 5).

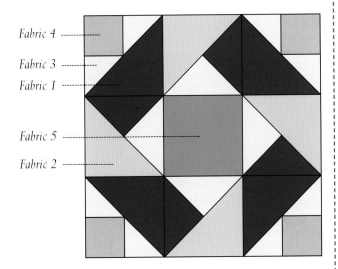

Fabric 4
Fabric 3
Fabric 1
Fabric 5
Fabric 2

MAKING THE QUILT

STEP 1:

Following the instructions on page 21, make the templates, adding a ¼-inch (6-mm) seam allowance all around on each shape.

STEP 2:

Using Template A, cut four patches from Fabric 1 and four from Fabric 2. Using Template B, cut four patches from Fabric 1 and four from Fabric 3. Using Template C, cut eight patches from Fabric 3. Using Template D, cut four patches from Fabric 4. Using Template E, cut one patch from Fabric 5.

STEP 3:

Join the patches to make the following units.

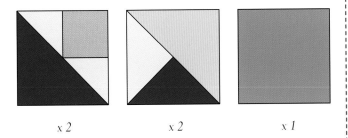

x 2   x 2   x 1

STEP 4:

Join the units as shown below to make a nine-patch block.

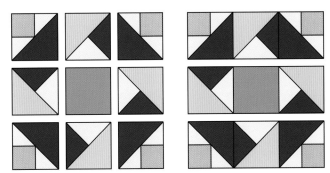

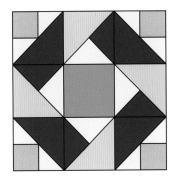

STEP 5:

Make the required number of blocks and join them together in rows to make the quilt.

STEP 6:

Complete the quilt top by adding plain borders (see page 32).

Completed Nine-Patch Weave quilt top, using nine blocks.

WEAVING AND TWISTING

Weaving and Twisting is a development of Nine-Patch Weave in which, once again, the illusion of interlacing is achieved by careful placement of the dark, medium, and light fabrics. Because every block is identical, once you've worked out your color scheme the rest is easy—but the resulting quilt will look impressively complex!

As for the Nine-Patch Weave, draft the pattern on an 18 x 18 square grid. Five templates are needed—A, B, C, D, and E.

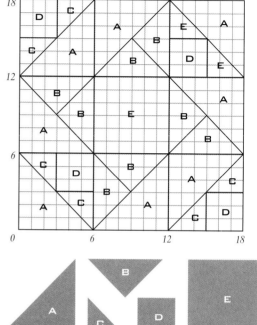

FABRICS

You will need five fabrics for this pattern—two dark fabrics (Fabrics 1 and 2), two medium fabrics (Fabric 3 and 4), and a light fabric (Fabric 5).

If you want to, you can vary the tones of your five fabrics to good effect. For example, in the quilt shown at the left, four different tones of purple have been used for Fabric 2. This has produced a transparent effect.

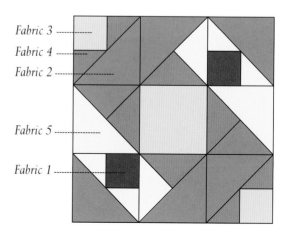

Fabric 3
Fabric 4
Fabric 2
Fabric 5
Fabric 1

MAKING THE QUILT

STEP 1:

Following the instructions on page 21, make templates A, B, C, D, and E, adding a ¼-inch (6-mm) seam allowance all around on each shape.

STEP 2:

Using Template A, cut six patches from Fabric 2 and two from Fabric 5. Using Template B, cut four patches from Fabric 4 and two each from Fabrics 2 and 5. Using Template C, cut four patches from Fabric 4 and four from Fabric 5. Using Template D, cut two patches from Fabric 1 and two from Fabric 3. Using Template E, cut one patch from Fabric 3.

STEP 3:

Taking a ¼-inch (6-mm) seam, piece the units as shown.

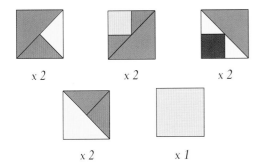

x 2   x 2   x 2

x 2   x 1

STEP 4:

Join the units into a nine-patch block, as shown below.

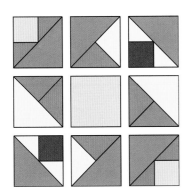

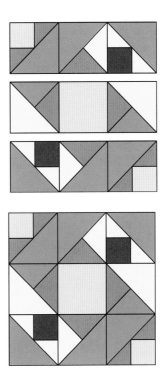

STEP 5:

Make the required number of blocks and join them together in rows to make the quilt.

Completed Weaving and Twisting quilt top using twelve blocks.

Draft the pattern on a 9 x 9 square grid. Only two templates are required—a half-square triangle (Template A), and a square (Template B).

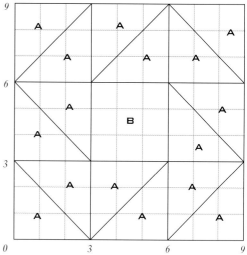

RIBBON STARS

Another nine-patch block, this pattern reveals stars between interweaving ribbons. Again, the effect of the pattern depends entirely on the color placement, but the ribbons can be either two tones of the same color or two different colors.

FABRICS

Four fabrics are needed for this pattern—a medium-dark fabric (Fabric 1), a dark fabric, (Fabric 2), a medium-light fabric (Fabric 3), and a light fabric (Fabric 4).

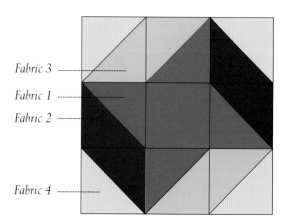

Fabric 3
Fabric 1
Fabric 2

Fabric 4

MAKING THE QUILT

STEP 1:

Following the drafting instructions on page 21, make Templates A and B, adding a ¼-inch (6-mm) seam allowance all around on each shape.

STEP 2:

Using Template A, cut four patches from each fabric. Using Template B, cut one patch from Fabric 1. (You can also make the patches for this pattern without using a template, using the rotary cutter method described on page 41.)

STEP 3:

Make the units as shown.

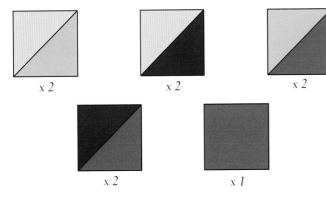

x 2   x 2   x 2

x 2   x 1

STEP 4:

Lay out the units as shown below and join them in rows into a nine-patch block.

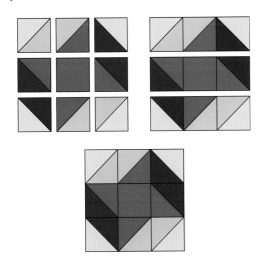

STEP 5:

Make the required number of blocks and join them together in rows.

STEP 6:

To finish, use the self-binding method shown on page 39.

Completed Ribbon Stars quilt top, using sixteen blocks.

RIBBON STARS VARIATION

An interesting variation is achieved simply by changing the color of the center square of each block.

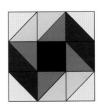

KENTUCKY CHAIN

Kentucky Chain was first published as a patchwork pattern in 1910 and it remains a popular way of creating an extremely complex-looking pattern from a quickly and easily pieced block.

The pattern is evolved from a single four-patch unit that is drafted on a 4 x 4 square grid. Four of these units are joined to form the block; the pattern appears when repeated blocks are set side by side in rows.

The illusion of interwoven bands depends entirely on the placement of the four colors, so care is needed in identifying the colors and their positions in the block. But once you've sorted that out, the rest is easy!

You will need three templates for this block.

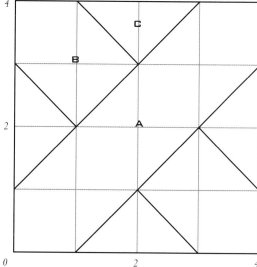

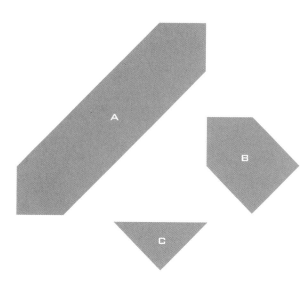

FABRICS

You need five fabrics for this pattern—a medium-dark fabric (Fabric 1), two medium-light fabrics (Fabrics 2 and 3), a medium-dark fabric (Fabric 4), and a dark fabric (Fabric 5).

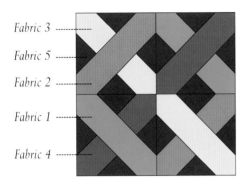

MAKING THE QUILT

STEP 1:

Following the drafting instructions on page 21, make Templates A, B, and C, adding a ¼-inch (6-mm) seam allowance all around on each shape.

STEP 2:

Using Template A, cut one patch each from Fabrics 1, 2, 3, and 4. Using Template B, cut two patches each from Fabrics 1, 2, 3, and 4. Using Template C, cut sixteen patches from Fabric 5.

STEP 3:

Piece the units as shown.

STEP 4:

Make one each of the four basic units.

STEP 5:

Join the units as shown below to make the block.

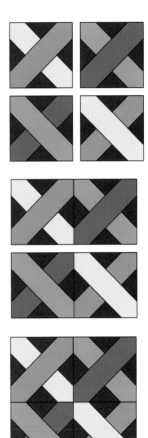

STEP 6:

Repeat and join the blocks in rows to make the quilt.

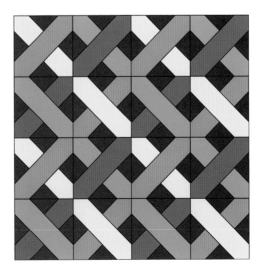

Completed Kentucky Chain quilt top, using four blocks.

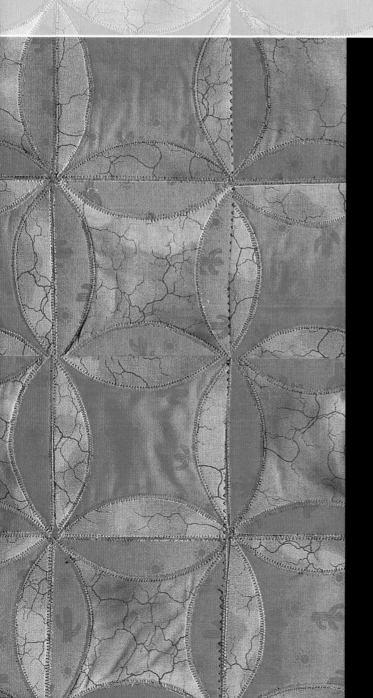

COUNTERCHANGE

The principle behind counterchange is that of interchangeable positive and negative shapes and colors. At first one color seems dominant, but the eye is soon diverted by the alternative interpretation of the pattern. In some patterns, two shapes may vie for attention, in which case the same pattern can produce two entirely different quilts when the respective light/dark values are exchanged. Many of the designs of the artist M.C. Escher are based on this principle.

Draft the pieced block on a 4 x 4 grid. Three templates—A, B, and C—are needed.

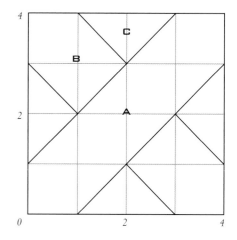

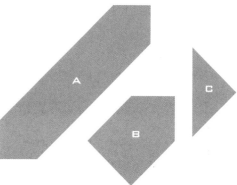

STAR CROSS

Seen on floor and wall tiles and on other decorative features such as screens, this is one of the most familiar of all Moorish patterns. Two distinct shapes—stars and crosses—appear, and the eye is constantly fooled into seeing first one and then the other. Further visual confusion arises when the viewer tries to work out how such a complex pattern is pieced. In fact, there is only one pieced block, which is alternated with plain blocks to create the illusion of eight-pointed stars and crosses. In practice, the pattern couldn't be easier to piece.

FABRICS

You will need two fabrics for the pieced block and a contrasting fabric for the unpieced block. Contrast is important, but it should not be so marked as to make one element of the pattern dominate the other completely. Dark, unpieced squares should be matched with medium-light crosses in a complementary color. The best effects are obtained by using small prints, which will hide the fact that four points of the star are actually part of the pieced block.

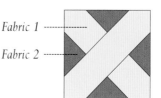

Fabric 1 -----------
Fabric 2 -----------

Pieced block   Un-pieced block

MAKING THE QUILT

STEP 1:

Following the instructions on page 21, make Templates A, B, and C, adding a ¼-inch (6-mm) seam allowance all around on each shape.

STEP 2:

Using Template A, cut one patch from Fabric 1. Using Template B, cut two patches from Fabric 1. Using Template C, cut four patches from Fabric 2.

STEP 3:

Piece two units as shown below.

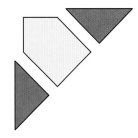 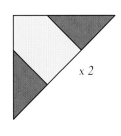

x 2

STEP 4:

Join the two units with a Template A patch.

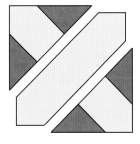 

STEP 5:

Cut the required number of squares from a contrasting fabric the same size as the pieced blocks.

STEP 6:

Following the diagram below, lay the blocks out "on point" (see page 31), alternating rows of solid and pieced blocks. Square off the pattern by adding part-blocks to the ends and corners. Note that the corner blocks are pieced in a different way to the full blocks.

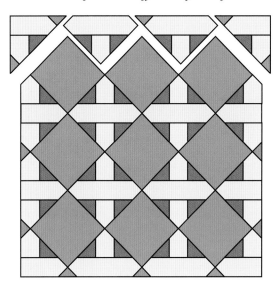

STEP 7:

To finish, add a double border—a plain dark border (see page 32), then a border with corner posts, in a fabric to complement the fabrics in the quilt.

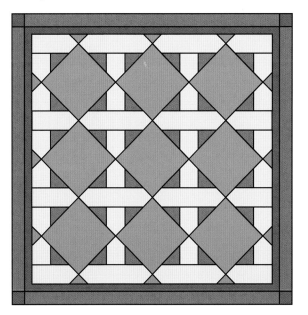

Completed Star Cross quilt top, using thirteen full blocks.

As with most counterchange patterns, the basic design is very simple and uses only two colors.

Draft the block on an 8 x 8 square grid, as shown below. Five templates are needed—A, B, C, D, and E.

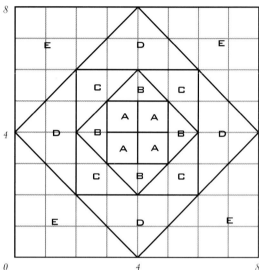

INDIANA PUZZLE

This pattern is also called Virginia Reel, Snail's Trail, and Monkey Wrench. It is a classic example of the counterchange illusion: Waves of two colors roll across the quilt surface, but the eye constantly changes focus from one color to the other. Which color is dominant? Look once and it's red; look again and it's black! An additional illusion is in the impression of curves, although only straight piecing is involved.

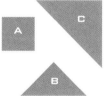
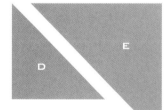

FABRICS
Only two fabrics are needed for this pattern. Choose colors with good, clear contrast. In the quilt shown, a pink and a black have been used.

Fabric 1 - - - - - - - - - - -

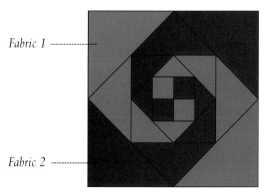

Fabric 2 - - - - - - - - - - -

MAKING THE QUILT

STEP 1:

Following the instructions on page 21, make Templates A, B, C, D, and E, adding a ¼-inch (6-mm) seam allowance all around on each shape.

STEP 2:

From each template, cut two patches in each fabric.

STEP 3:

Working from the center of the block, piece the center unit as shown.

STEP 4:

Add Template B triangles to all four sides of the center unit, noting the color placement.

STEP 5:

Add Template C triangles to all four sides.

STEP 6:

Add Template D triangles to all four sides.

 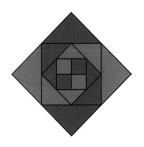

STEP 7:

Add Template E triangles to complete the block.

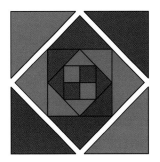 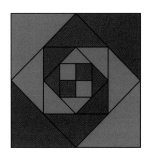

STEP 8:

Join the blocks and finish by binding (see page 38).

Completed Indiana Puzzle quilt top, using sixteen blocks.

INDIANA PUZZLE VARIATION

In this quilt, alternate blocks have been rotated by 45 degrees, producing a completely different counterchange effect.

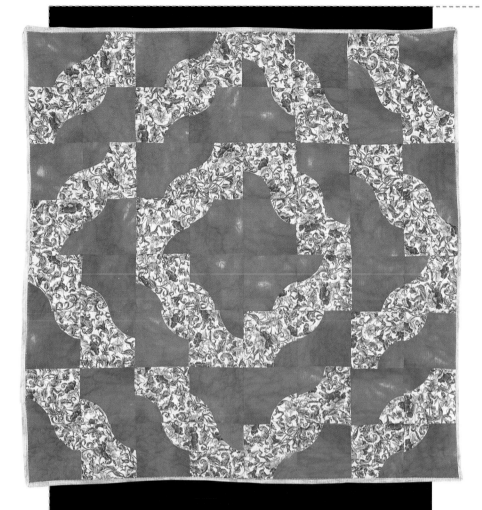

This is a very simple block to construct, although care is needed in piecing the curved patches.

Two templates —A and B—are needed. Instructions for drafting a 6 x 6-inch (15 x 15-cm) block are given on page 23.

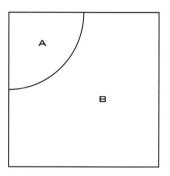

FABRICS

Two fabrics are needed. The pattern works well as a monochrome quilt, if there is enough contrast between the tones of the color chosen. Alternatively, choose two different colors that complement each other well.

DRUNKARD'S PATH

This pattern is also called Fool's Puzzle, Falling Timbers, Country Husband, and Solomon's Puzzle. There are many variations on this traditional block, which is constructed from a basic unit of two patches and two fabrics. These blocks can be arranged in many ways to create a variety of quilt patterns. In the quilt shown, although the blocks have been rotated to echo a barn-raising design, the disjointed lines disrupt this interpretation and constantly invite the eye to settle on another one.

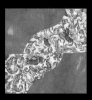

MAKING THE QUILT

STEP 1:

Follow the instructions on page 23 for drafting the block using a compass. To make the templates, trace the shapes onto template plastic or cardboard, adding a ¼-inch (6-mm) seam allowance all around on each shape.

STEP 2:

From each template, cut thirty-two patches in each fabric.

STEP 3:

Piece each block as shown, following the instructions on page 28 for sewing curves.

Block A

Block B

STEP 4:

Lay out the blocks row by row, following the diagram below.

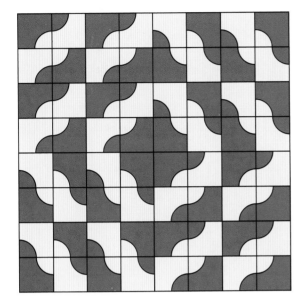

STEP 5:

Finish the quilt by binding or butting (see page 38).

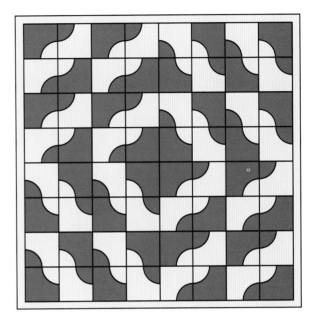

Completed quilt top, using sixty-four blocks.

SNOWBALL VARIATION

In this version, alternate color groups are set opposite each other, producing an interesting pattern of checkerboards with two-colored circles at the junctions.

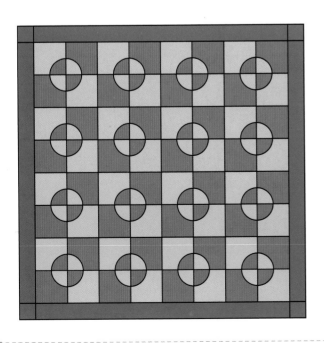

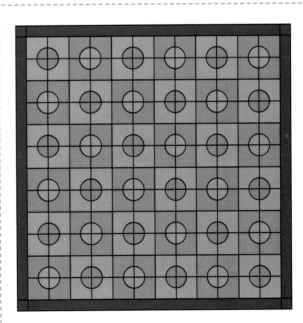

POLKA DOT VARIATION

Here, blocks made from four patches in one color group are alternated with blocks made from the other color group, resulting in a lively polka dot pattern.

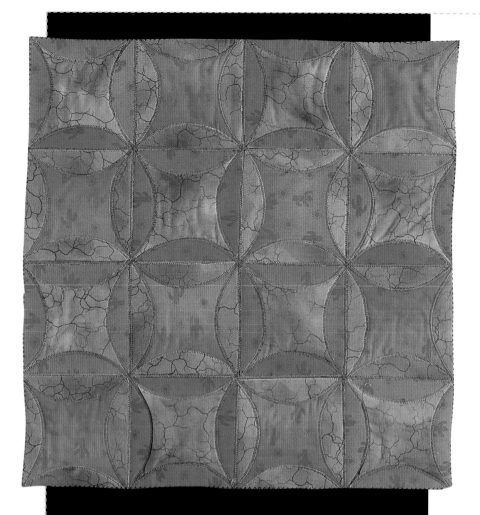

The pattern can be pieced in the conventional way, but this is definitely one for which the much easier fusible webbing appliqué method described here is recommended. For this, only one template, a shallow curve with one straight edge, is needed. Instructions for drafting a 6 x 6-inch (15 x 15-cm) block for this quilt are given on page 22.

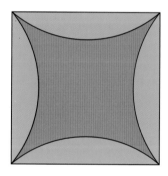

The pattern is created by making blocks in two color groups and laying them out alternately on the quilt top.

Block A

Block B

ROBBING PETER TO PAY PAUL

Taking a small crescent from each side of a block of one color and interchanging it with a crescent from a block of another color results in a complex eye-fooler pattern. In this quilt, both turquoise and orange circles are seen. Within each circle, a curve-sided square of one color appears to be lying on top of a square of the other color.

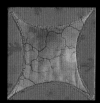

FABRICS

You will need only two fabrics for this quilt. Bright, zingy colors with good contrast work best for this pattern.

MAKING THE QUILT

STEP 1:

Follow the instructions on page 22 for drafting the block using a compass.

STEP 2:

To make the templates, trace the drafted shapes onto template plastic or cardboard. Cut out each shape without adding a seam allowance.

STEP 3:

Cut an even number of squares from each fabric, adding a ¼-inch (6-mm) seam allowance all around the square. Using a ruler and a 2B (#2) pencil, mark the seam allowance on all sides of the square.

STEP 4:

Iron fusible webbing to the wrong side of the fabrics. Using the template and a 2B (#2) pencil, mark out four curved patches from the contrasting color for each square.

STEP 5:

Cut out the patches. Peel off the paper and iron the patches onto the background squares. Apply the curved patches from one color to the square of the other color, positioning the straight edge of the curved patch exactly on the marked seam allowance.

STEP 6:

When the blocks are finished, stitch around the curves, using a narrow zig-zag stitch, to seal and cover the joined edges.

STEP 7:

Complete the quilt top by joining the blocks in rows, alternating Blocks A and B.

STEP 8:

Finish the quilt with butted edges (see page 38), or add plain borders (see page 33).

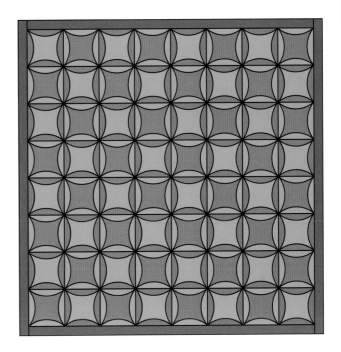

Completed Robbing Peter to Pay Paul quilt top with plain borders, using sixty-four blocks.

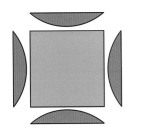
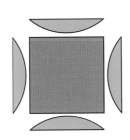
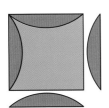
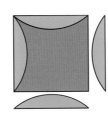

To piece this bock the conventional way, two templates are needed—A and B. Instructions for drafting a 6 x 6-inch (15 x 15-cm) block for this quilt are given on page 23.

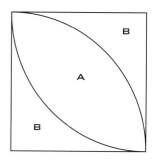

FABRICS

You will need two fabrics that contrast well with one another.

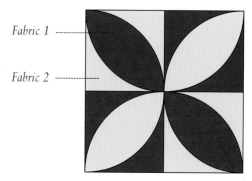

Fabric 1 ----------

Fabric 2 ----------

MELON PATCH

The curved petal shapes on Melon Patch add to the optical quandary of this example of counterchange: In addition to the puzzle of which color group to focus on, there are the two-color circles formed by the petals, and the curved-sided squares between them. As with most counterchange patterns, the construction of the blocks is extremely simple. It can be made even simpler by using either hand or machine appliqué for the petals.

MAKING THE QUILT

STEP 1:

Follow the instructions on page 23 for drafting the block using a compass. To make the templates, trace the shapes onto template plastic or cardboard, adding a ¼-inch (6-mm) seam allowance all around each shape.

STEP 2:

Using Template A, cut two patches from Fabric 1 and two from Fabric 2.

STEP 3:

Using Template B, cut four patches from Fabric 1 and four from Fabric 2.

STEP 4:

Following the instructions on page 28 for sewing curves, piece the units as shown below.

x 2   *x 2*

STEP 5:

Join the units to make the block.

STEP 6:

To complete the quilt top, join the required number of blocks together. Add a plain border, following the instructions on page 32.

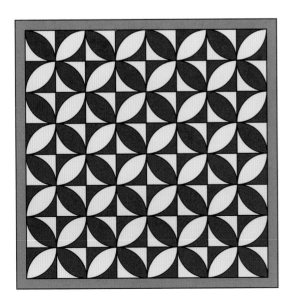

Completed Melon Patch quilt top, using sixteeen blocks.

MELON PATCH VARIATION

In this intriguingly complex variation on the Melon Patch block, each petal is divided in two, which, in turn, means that the colors of surrounding patches must be similarly alternated.

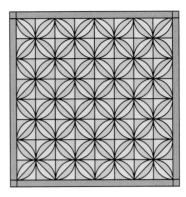

MAKING THE BLOCK

STEP 1:

Draft the block exactly as for Melon Patch, but divide Template A into two halves. Use one half as the new template, remembering to add ¼ inch (6 mm) all around for the seam allowance.

STEP 2:

Using the Template, cut four patches from Fabric 1 and four from Fabric 2.

STEP 3:

Join a Fabric 1 patch to a Fabric 2 patch to make the petal.

STEP 4:

Using Template B, cut four patches from Fabric 1 and four from Fabric 2.

STEP 5:

Make the two units as shown.

STEP 6:

Join the units to complete the block.

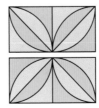 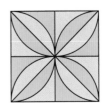

TRANSPARENCY

An illusion of transpareny is created that one fabric is physically laid over another so that the lower fabric appears to show through to the surface. There are two ways to create effects of transparency. You can choose two colors plus a darker version of one of them for the area where they appear to overlap or you can use colors that are next to each other on the color wheel (analogous colors) in such a way as to suggest overlapping.

The block is made by the appliqué method; hand or machine appliqué can be used. The fusible-webbing method (see page 115) also works well. Instructions for making the block by this method are given below.

Only three templates—A, B, and C—are needed for the shapes, which are applied to a background square. Instructions for drafting a 12 x 12-inch (30 x 30-cm) block for this quilt are given on page 23.

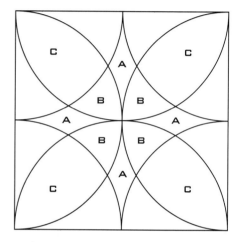

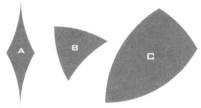

FABRICS

This quilt has been made using four fabrics—dark purple (Fabric 1), purple (Fabric 2), and pink (Fabric 3) for the appliqué shapes, plus cream (Fabric 4) for the background square, but other combinations will work as well. See the guidelines on page 8 for choosing fabrics for transparency effects.

ALABAMA BEAUTY

Adapted from the traditional Alabama Beauty block, four of these blocks make an effective wall hanging. The four petal shapes appear to overlap the curve-sided square in the middle. The overlap appears to show through as a mixture of the two colors.

Fabric 1 --------
Fabric 2 --------
Fabric 4 --------
Fabric 3 --------

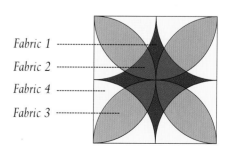

MAKING THE QUILT

STEP 1:

Follow the instructions on page 23 for drafting the block using a compass. To make the templates, trace the shapes onto template plastic or cardboard. Cut out each shape without adding a seam allowance.

STEP 2:

Cut out the background square. Using a ruler and a 2B (#2) pencil, mark the ¼-inch (6-mm) seam allowance on all sides of the square. Fold it in half and press well. Open it out, fold it in the other direction, and press again. Open it out, fold it diagonally, and press. Open it out again, fold it diagonally in the other direction, and press.

STEP 3:

Using a moderately hot iron, apply fusible webbing to the wrong side of each fabric. On the paper backing of the fusible webbing, draw around the templates the required number of times and cut out the patches. You need four Template A patches from Fabric 1, four Template B patches from Fabric 2, and four Template C patches from Fabric 3. The patches are now ready to be applied to the background fabric.

STEP 4:

Remove the paper backing and start ironing shapes onto the background square (Fabric 4), working from the center outward and using the fold lines as a guide. Position the patches at the four corners inside the marked seam allowance. Apply Fabric 2 patches first, then Fabric 1, and finally Fabric 3.

STEP 5:

When the appliqué is complete, anchor the patches with narrow zig-zag stitches to cover the edges, using thread that blends well with one or both of the adjoining patches.

STEP 6:

Complete the quilt top by adding a narrow border (see page 32).

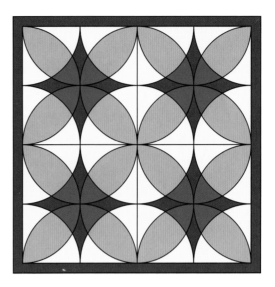

Completed Alabama Beauty quilt top. The transparency effect is created by patches that appear to be overlapping.

ALABAMA BEAUTY REPEATED

Repeated Alabama Beauty blocks make a particularly striking quilt as, in addition to the transparency effect, the repeated blocks reveal a pattern of circles.

Alabama Beauty quilt top, with border, using sixteen blocks.

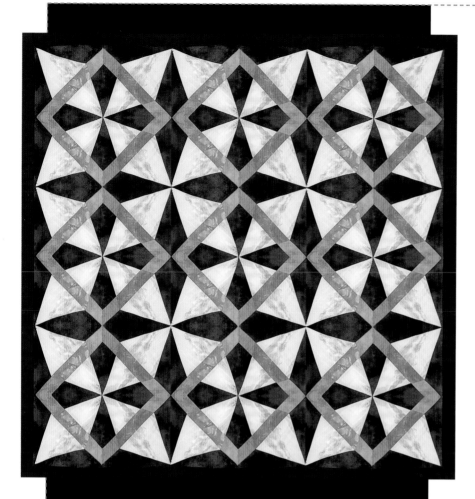

This block is drafted on an 8 x 8 square grid. In its original form, the long diamonds cross over the diagonally placed square (Block A). To create the transparency, redraft the block, identifying the patches where the two elements of the pattern overlap (Block B).

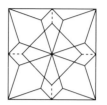 

Block A

Block B

In Block B, the dark pink shapes cross the blue diamond, and the two colors combine to produce purple. Other combinations—for example, yellow shapes over blue diamonds meeting as green—could be used as well. To make the transparent version of Barbara Bannister Star, six templates are needed.

BARBARA BANNISTER STAR

Many pieced blocks in which patches can be seen to overlay other shapes lend themselves well to adaptation for transparency effects. Barbara Bannister Star is a good example of this.

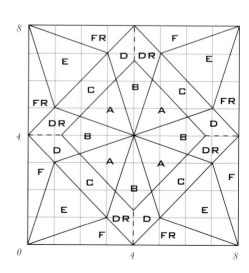

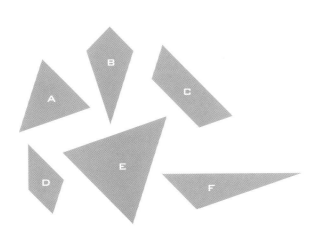

FABRICS

The choice of fabrics is extremely important in transparency projects. Other color groups could be used to produce the same effect (see page 119), but this quilt has been made using four fabrics—blue (Fabric 1), purple (Fabric 2), pink (Fabric 3), and black (Fabric 4).

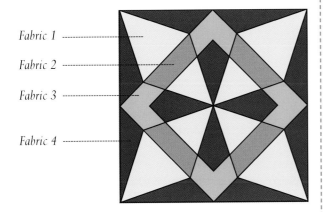

Fabric 1

Fabric 2

Fabric 3

Fabric 4

MAKING THE QUILT

STEP 1:

Following the instructions on page 21, make the templates, adding a ¼-inch (6-mm) seam allowance all around on each shape.

STEP 2:

Using Template A, cut four patches from Fabric 1. Using Template B, cut four patches from Fabric 4. Using Template C, cut four patches from Fabric 2. Using Template D, cut four patches from Fabric 3, then reverse the Template and cut four more. Using Template E, cut four patches from Fabric 1. Using Template F, cut four patches from Fabric 4, then reverse the Template and cut four more.

STEP 3:

Join the Template A and B patches to make the center square.

STEP 4:

Piece the corner units.

STEP 5:

Join the corner units to the center square.

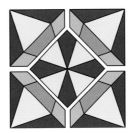 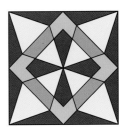

STEP 6:

Join the required number of blocks together and add a plain border (see page 32) to complete the quilt.

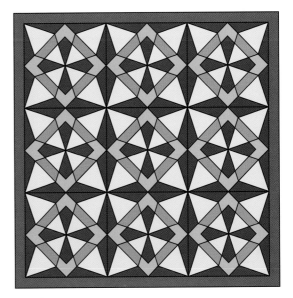

Completed Barbara Bannister Star quilt top. Blue octagons appear around four-pointed black stars, combining with the transparency illusion to create a beautiful eye-fooler quilt.

When set side by side, the Star and Chains blocks produce even more transparency effects as the diagonal bands on the block join up to form squares, enhancing the visual impact of the block.

Although the piecing needs care, and is most easily done by hand using the English patchwork method (see page 26), the beauty of the effects obtained amply repays the effort.

The block is drafted on a 14 x 14 square grid. Five templates are needed—A, B, C, D, and E.

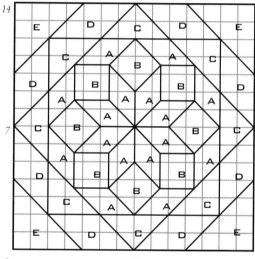

STAR AND CHAINS

This quilt is made from four blocks of Star and Chains, which is one of the many mosaic blocks first published toward the end of the nineteenth century. An intricately pieced square appears to be set on top of a lighter-colored square that is set on point beneath it. The red diamonds set at angles around the center design represent the chains.

FABRICS

As with all transparency projects, the choice of fabrics is the decisive factor in achieving the desired effects. In the block used for this quilt, the eye is invited to see the bright red patches as part of a complete square, the corners of which are black because they overlap the darker red bands around the block. Other color groups could be used to produce the same effect.

To create this block you will need five fabrics—a medium-dark blue (Fabric 1), a light blue (Fabric 2), black (Fabric 3), bright red (Fabric 4), and a medium-dark red (Fabric 5).

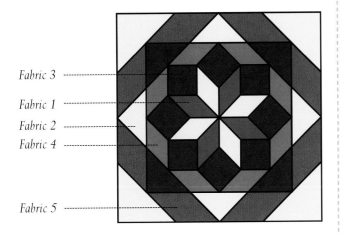

Fabric 3
Fabric 1
Fabric 2
Fabric 4

Fabric 5

MAKING THE QUILT

STEP 1:

Following the instructions on page 21, make master Templates A, B, C, D, and E without adding a seam allowance. Cut paper templates using the master templates.

STEP 2:

Using Template A, cut four patches from Fabric 1, four from Fabric 2, and eight from Fabric 4. Using Template B, cut eight patches from Fabric 3. Using Template C, cut four patches from Fabric 2 and four from Fabric 3. Using Template D, cut eight patches from Fabric 5. Using Template E, cut four patches from Fabric 2. Add a ¼-inch (6-mm) seam allowance all around on each shape.

STEP 3:

Baste patches over paper, turning under at the corners, as shown on page 26.

STEP 4:

When all the patches have been basted, piece the block as shown. Join all patches by overstitiching seams.

STEP 5:

Press the patchwork gently but firmly on the front, then take out the basting stitches and remove the papers. Leave the edges of the patches at the sides of the block turned under.

STEP 6:

To make the quilt, join the blocks in rows. Add mitered borders following the English patchwork method on page 33.

Completed Star and Chains quilt top with mitered borders, using four blocks.

GLOSSARY

BACKING
The bottom layer of the quilt, under the top and batting.

BALANCE MARKS
Points marked on adjacent patches to be matched when stitching curves. Also known as "notches."

BASTING
Large running stitches used to hold two or more layers in position before final sewing or quilting.

BATTING
The layer placed between the quilt top and the backing.

BINDING
A method of finishing raw edges around the sides of the quilt by enclosing them in strips of folded fabric.

BUTTING
A method of finishing edges by turning them in toward each other.

COMPASS
Mathematical instrument for drawing curves and circles.

COUNTERCHANGE
Reversing colors on a pattern to emphasize negative and positive shapes.

ENGLISH PATCHWORK
A method of making patchwork by basting fabric over papers, then whipstitching the seams by hand.

FREEZER PAPER
Thick white paper that can be ironed on to fabric as a temporary stitching guide. Useful for appliqué.

FUSIBLE WEBBING
Paper with adhesive on one side; used for appliqué.

GEOMETRIC
Mathematical proportioning of shapes, lines, angles, points, surfaces, and solids.

GRID
A pattern of horizontal and vertical lines.

HUE
Color as it is percieved—for example, blue, red.

ISOMETRIC GRID
A grid based on 60-degree triangles. Hexagons, six-pointed stars, and other patterns based on that angle are drafted on this type of grid.

INTENSITY
A term that describes the brightness, depth, and impact of a color.

INTERLACING
The appearance of strands going under and over each other, as in weaving.

MITERING
Technique for finishing quilt borders to resemble picture frames.

MOSAIC PATCHWORK
Alternative name for English patchwork, reflecting the complex patterns, resembling mosaic floor-tiles, that can be pieced by this method.

MUSLIN
Plain-woven, natural-colored cotton. Sold in varying qualities, from fine to heavyweight.

POSTS
Square patches set where sashing strips meet.

SASHING
Strips set between quilt blocks, usually of a contrasting color.

SHADE
Dark values of a pure color, resulting from the addition of black.

THREE-DIMENSIONAL (3D)
The appearance of depth.

TINT
Light value of a color, achieved by the addition of white.

TONE
Values of gray, produced by mixing black and white to the pure color.

TRANSPARENCY
The effect created by overlapping two or more colors in such a way that underlying colors appear to show through.

INDEX

FURTHER READING

Albers, J.

INTERACTION OF COLOR

(New Haven, CT: Yale University Press, 1971).
A classic text on the subject of color.

Beyer, J.

PATCHWORK PATTERNS

(McLean, VA: EPM Publications, 1979).
Basic pattern drafting of traditional blocks.

Fisher, L.

QUILTS OF ILLUSION

(London: Blandford, 1990).
The extraordinary optical effects of many traditional patterns explained and illustrated, with patterns and templates to make some of them.

Holstein, J.

THE PIECED QUILT: AN AMERICAN DESIGN TRADITION

(New York: New York Graphic Society, 1973).
The definitive account of the history, traditions, and significance of the American patchwork quilt. The author is credited with the 1970s revival of interest in the quilt and quiltmaking, as both art and craft, which led to the contemporary boom.

Itten, J.

THE ART OF COLOR

(New York: Van Nostrand Reinhold Co., 1969).

James, M.

THE QUILTMAKER'S HANDBOOK

(Englewood Cliffs, NJ: Prentice-Hall, 1978).
After more than twenty years, this is still one of the best and most comprehensive guides to design, technique, and color, with very thorough and detailed "how-to" instructions. Includes guides to designing and drafting your own blocks and making and using templates.

James, M.

THE SECOND QUILTMAKER'S HANDBOOK

(Englewood Cliffs, NJ: Prentice-Hall, 1981).
Advanced advice and instruction on design and practical quiltmaking; a sequel to the author's first book.

Kritchlow, K.

ISLAMIC PATTERNS

(London: Thames and Hudson, 1976).
A scholarly but accessible explanation of both the philosophy and the mathematical principles that underlie Islamic patterns.

Stockton, J.

DESIGNER'S GUIDE TO COLOR

(San Francisco: Chronicle Books, 1984 [3 vols]).
An indispensable practical guide to using color and color combinations.

CREDITS

The piecing method for "Oriental Star" is used with permission of the copyright holder, the Estate of the late Margit Echols. Sincere thanks to David Tofani.

Quilts made by Debbie Woolley and Celia Eddy, except "Kaleidoscope" by Margaret Briggs, to whom grateful thanks is given.

Thanks to Debbie Woolley for also providing invaluable help and advice on fabric choices and for quilting and finishing many of the quilts, and to Julie Huck for modeling for the step-by-step photography.

All photographs and illustrations are the copyright of Quarto Publishing plc. While every effort has been made to credit contributors, Quarto would like to apologise should there have been any omissions or errors.